heartwood

heartwood

THE ART OF

LIVING WITH

THE END IN MIND

Barbara Becker

FLATIRON
BOOKS
NEW YORK

HEARTWOOD. Copyright © 2021 by Barbara Becker. All rights reserved. Printed in the United States of America. For information, address Flatiron Books, 120 Broadway, New York, NY 10271.

Unless otherwise noted, all photographs courtesy of the author

Illustrations of tree rings courtesy of Ekaterina Bodyagina/ Shutterstock.com

A version of "Marisa" originally appeared on *Modern Loss*. Republished here with permission.

A version of "Felix" originally appeared in *Salon*.

www.flatironbooks.com

Designed by Donna Sinisgalli Noetzel

Library of Congress Cataloging-in-Publication Data

Names: Becker, Barbara (Barbara Anne), 1967– author.
Title: Heartwood : the art of living with the end in mind / Barbara Becker.
Description: First edition. | New York : Flatiron Books, 2021. | Includes bibliographical references.
Identifiers: LCCN 2020053244 | ISBN 9781250095985 (hardcover) | ISBN 9781250095992 (ebook)
Subjects: LCSH: Becker, Barbara (Barbara Anne), 1967—Family. | Becker, Barbara (Barbara Anne), 1967—Friends and associates. | Death—Social aspects. | Terminally ill—Anecdotes. | Grief—Anecdotes.
Classification: LCC HQ1073 .B425 2021 | DDC 306.9—dc23
LC record available at https://lccn.loc.gov/2020053244

Our books may be purchased in bulk for promotional, educational, or business use. Please contact your local bookseller or the Macmillan Corporate and Premium Sales Department at 1-800-221-7945, extension 5442, or by email at MacmillanSpecialMarkets@macmillan.com.

First Edition: 2021

10 9 8 7 6 5 4 3 2 1

To

George and Alice Becker

My heartwood

Dave, Evan, and Drew

My growth rings

contents

heartwood

\ ˈhärt-ˌwu̇d\

noun

1 the older harder nonliving central wood of trees that is usually darker, denser, less permeable, and more durable than the surrounding sapwood (Merriam-Webster)

2 a teaching by the Buddha comparing the layers of a tree—the twigs and leaves, outer bark, inner bark, sapwood—to the spiritual discoveries that may distract a seeker before they come to realize the unshakable deliverance of mind, or "heartwood" (*Mahasaropama Sutta,* or "The Greater Discourse on the Simile of the Heartwood")

3 a reminder to embrace the inseparability of life and death, the growth rings and the heartwood . . . a message of wholeness (Author)

author's note

I meant to write about death, only life came breaking in as usual, Virginia Woolf wrote in her diary on February 17, 1922. Oh, how I understood her, for I too had set out to write about death.

In my early life, after learning that someone had to die for me to live, death had slipped quietly into my home and declared herself my teacher. Her initial appearance was more gentle than wrenching, and I was open, the first stirrings of curiosity in my young life. "Nothing is required but that you pay careful attention," she seemed to say. Later, I feared, loathed, and resented her deeply, though I never stopped sensing that there were things of great significance to be witnessed. But what is to be learned from death? How was I supposed to make myself available to listen? And what was I supposed to do with these understandings in the practical, brass-tacks way of a modern woman going about her daily business?

There were stories I wanted to tell, people I wanted to honor, things she had whispered to me that I longed to give voice to through writing. My friends Nancy and Jordan loaned me their house at the beach in New Jersey for a few days so I could find the silence I never had in my city apartment, so full of adolescent-boy energy that I only half-jokingly referred to it as the frat house.

It was early March, decidedly not beach weather. I set up my computer at Nancy's desk overlooking the ocean and raised the blinds. Sun reflected off the water, beach grass blew southward like a line of schoolgirls' long hair swept in the wind, and a pair of mourning doves cooed on the telephone wire outside the window. In all of ten minutes, I closed the cover of my laptop, pulled on my winter coat and woolen hat, and raced outside to join in the symphony of life.

My paternal grandparents had grown up in this Victorian town along the New Jersey shore. I cannot walk the boardwalk without catching a sense of them, dressed in the modest black one-piece bathing suits that women and men alike wore in the 1920s. I can see my father as a child on the merry-go-round, its ornate pavilion now off-limits behind chain-link fencing and a secure lock.

I remember my mother's mother, age eighty though child-like in her dementia, asking to see the ocean one last time. How my mother and I had bundled her into the car and driven an hour and a half to the boardwalk. We fed her bites of funnel cake sprinkled with powdered sugar on a bench under a gazebo and then spent an hour in the public toilet cleaning her up after it disagreed with her. The next day, back at home, she looked at us—our excursion already forgotten—and said, "Boy, I'd really like to go the shore one last time."

And I remember my childhood friend Marisa sitting at the

water's edge as we built a sandcastle, patiently letting droplets of wet sand fall from our cupped hands, one by one, until we had towering spires to rival anything Gaudí could have imagined.

All of these people, these great loves in my life, are now gone. I miss each of them. Sometimes still I wake in tears. This aching grief is part of the journey, I have learned, on no one's timetable but my own. But there's something else, an enlivening essence that remains after every death, every departure. All of these people—my grandparents, my parents, Marisa, and other dear ones—have become part of my heartwood.

Heartwood. In the poetry of nature, I encountered a metaphor of loss and life, hand in hand, enhancing one another. Inland from the coast are acres of forests where I first learned of its existence. If you have the chance to examine the cross section of a tree, you will notice a central core, darker than the sapwood surrounding it. Called heartwood, this supporting pillar no longer participates in the life process of a tree—transporting and storing water and nutrients. Although dead, heartwood will not decay or lose its sturdiness while the outer, living rings of newer growth sustain it. In the perfect ecology of a tree, the dead become the heart of the living, and the living nourish the enduring essence of the dead.

So it is with our lives, where life and death cannot exist separately from each other. Heartwood is about strength in what remains and the virtue of listening to our innermost source of stability and stillness. It is about how trusting the natural cycle of life and loss can help us to better live our lives. It applies equally in ordinary times as it does during the most trying of times, when the surety of our existence is called into question.

I have learned that being open to death is a powerful way to learn about living. That when we stop pretending we will live forever, a certain tightness begins to loosen. Slowly, as we give ourselves permission to relax the vise grip we use to try to control our circumstances, a sense of freedom emerges from within. Though little may have changed on the outside, and loss will continue to be our companion, our internal landscape is renewed. Just as we will cherish ourselves more, we will cherish others more as well. Sometimes, as the great masters have taught, we have to die before we die if we want to truly live.

heartwood

MARISA

Statistically my time was up at least a year ago. But I'm still here, wrote my childhood friend Marisa at the top of her Facebook note titled *25 Random Things About Me.* I had read and reread her list so many times I'd nearly committed it to memory.

Marisa and I met the day her family moved onto our street in suburban New Jersey. She was the curly-haired little sister in a gregarious Italian Catholic family. I was a stringy-haired bookworm—the oldest sibling in a family of reserved Protestants. Her brother was inseparable from my brothers, and our parents barbecued together while we played hide-and-seek in the woods on summer nights.

Marisa discovered the marble-sized mass in her left breast ten months before her wedding to her college sweetheart, David. She was thirty. After a lumpectomy, a dozen rounds of chemotherapy, and thirty radiation sessions, Marisa and David said their vows while my mother passed a packet of tissues down the church pew. They donated a portion of their wedding gifts to cancer research and settled into a tidy brick home on Philadelphia's Main Line.

Meanwhile, I had married my own David. We had two sons

and lived in a New York City apartment cluttered with books and toys. We were hectic but happy. I saw Marisa at our families' annual Christmas dinners in New Jersey; mostly we kept in touch online.

By the time Marisa was thirty-nine, the cancer was in her liver, spine, skull, ribs, hip, and lymph nodes. She responded by focusing on what gave her joy. Small things, like #12 of her Facebook *Random Things* list—*I'm addicted to Us Weekly*—and #15's *Raisinets*. David's love warranted two entries: #6—*I think my husband is the funniest person I know. And the most loyal*—and #25—*I believe my husband and I were truly meant for each other.*

Marisa's struggle made me profoundly unsettled. After reading her list for the first time, I began waking up at 3 A.M., trying to catch my breath. In our darkened bedroom, I'd sit against the headboard, knees pulled up to my chest, and think about mortality—Marisa's and my own.

To ease the anxiety, I read. I devoured so many books about life's purpose that my husband began shaking his head every time I came home from the library with a new one. As a young girl, I had taken an uncanny interest in my father's colorful six-book set on world religions (Buddhism, Hinduism, Islam, Judaism, Catholicism, and Protestantism), which opened a vast and exhilarating universe of beliefs and rituals that existed beyond our small town. He had told me he bought the set so he could learn more about his colleagues at the local hospital, who came from all over the globe. Now, as if channeling my younger self,

I began to search broadly for words of wisdom on life, death, and meaning. I discovered that seekers and sages from Henry David Thoreau to the mystical poet Rumi to the Dalai Lama have long implored us to live with the end ever-present in our minds. A review of scientific studies claimed that thinking about mortality could actually be good for re-prioritizing goals and values. Even Apple's Steve Jobs asserted, *Death is very likely the single best invention of Life. It is Life's change agent.*

In a move I thought would make Marisa's playful eyes roll—that is, if I had told her about it—I decided to test this wisdom by living a year of my life as if it were my last. While I was not in the habit of praying, each morning I would close my eyes and dedicate my experiment to Marisa. Then I would fill in the blank: *I don't want to die without . . .*

After Marisa wrote to tell me how ecstatic she was about a family vacation in Italy she had taken between chemo sessions, I booked a trip to Turkey, which I had been putting off until my kids were older. Hadn't I read that people often go to their end regretting things they did *not* do far more than regretting some of the things they *did* do? I was determined not to make that mistake. In Istanbul, Dave, the boys, and I drank fresh-squeezed pomegranate juice on cobblestone streets and watched the whirling dervishes spin into a trance—one outstretched palm turned upward to receive graces from the heavens, the other facing downward to pass them on to earth.

Next, I tackled work. I used my flexibility as a strategic-communications consultant to develop a pro-bono campaign for refugees in North Africa. My income shrank, but my days felt purposeful. I went on a ten-day silent meditation retreat, planted tulip and daffodil bulbs in a sooty plot in the shade of the Williamsburg Bridge, and snapped at my kids less, imagining each interaction could be our last. Dave and I held hands watching *Saturday Night Live* reruns.

Slowly I understood that my quest was an invitation to participate more fully in everyday matters. While I had initially been looking for meaning along the banks of the Bosporus Strait in Istanbul, answers were just as easily found in my newly flowering garden, where elevated trains rumbled on tracks overhead. Meditating at home on a floor strewn with Legos felt even more useful than sitting on a perfectly aligned cushion in a serene hall. I cried openly and often for Marisa and her family and in gratitude for her unwitting gift to me.

Toward the end of my 365-day experiment, Marisa's doctors told her there was nothing more they could do. I arranged a babysitter and drove to her parents' house, where she was staying. "You might think sitting with someone who is dying means you will be having big conversations about the meaning of life," a hospice chaplain had advised me. "Wrong! Sometimes, all that's called for is to just show up and watch *Jeopardy!* together."

I found Marisa lying on the couch, staring at the TV, which was off. She turned to greet me, her voice thin and ethereal, caused by tumors covering her larynx. We fell into an easy recitation of our childhood stories. How we had allowed our brothers to zoom bikes off a ramp and over us à la Evel

Marisa (left) and me
Long Beach Island, New Jersey

Knievel as we lay on the asphalt, holding our breath. The summer her family rented a Winnebago and, deciding that campsites weren't for them, parked it in the driveway of our rental house at the beach.

"Every big childhood memory involves you," she said, her eyelids heavy.

"I know you'll get b—" I began to lie, but then closed my mouth.

I took a slight step back. She looked older than her forty years. Her hair was now short and patchy, her skin ashen gray.

I desperately wanted something extraordinary to happen—a pearl of wisdom to be uttered, a *deus ex machina* to appear. But in that same sunlit room where we had spent countless hours playing as kids, everything felt still and ordinary. In what was to be our last moment together, we leaned forward to touch foreheads, as always.

Marisa died five days after my year-to-live experiment came to an end.

MAUREEN

I grew up in a home that was frequented by a ghost.

I was eight years old when I first encountered her. That day, as I walked down the long, carpeted hallway of our ranch house, I noticed that my father had left his wallet on the dresser in his and my mother's bedroom. Knowing he was outside raking leaves and my mother was grocery shopping, I tiptoed in, picked it up, and with only the slightest hesitation, opened the weathered leather fold. Inside were a few bills, a photo of my brothers and me, and another of my mother, in a starched nurse's cap, smiling broadly.

I was about to put the wallet down when I noticed the frayed edge of another picture behind that of my mother.

Gently, I pulled at it until it came free. A pretty woman peered back at me from the black-and-white photo. She was younger than my mother, in a cardigan sweater, with blond hair swept back in a soft bun. She looked friendly, like someone you'd want to meet.

I'm not sure how long I stood there staring at the image of the woman, trying to compute who she was and why she was in my father's wallet. I was so absorbed that I didn't hear the garage door open and my mother come into the house until she was standing directly behind me.

"Oh, Annie," she said, looking from the photo to me and calling me by a name only she and my father have ever used.

"Who is this?" I asked, a need-to-know indignance winning out over the embarrassment of being caught red-handed in the act of snooping.

She sighed and sat down on the edge of the bed. "That was Maureen," she said. "Your father's first wife."

My father was a medical resident at Yale University, busy pulling all-nighters and surviving on shredded wheat, when he found out that he had been selected to spend a rotation in London studying the pioneering work emerging in the field of neurosurgery. He jumped at the opportunity. His roommate in London was another Yale student, Sherwin "Shep" Nuland, who would later, and rather synchronously, enter my life not only as my father's friend but also as the author of an unflinching book on what happens to the human body at the end of life, called *How We Die.* But I am getting ahead of myself.

Maureen was a twenty-one-year-old British nurse, working in the radiology department of the same Queen Square hospital, specializing in brain tumors and head trauma. She was bright, joyful, and a willing guide around town for the American doctor. She took my father to her home outside London to meet her parents, who called her their English Rose. It wasn't long before they had fallen in love.

My father and Maureen married in a small ceremony in a picturesque Anglican parish church near her childhood home, where an ancient yew tree—a species long associated with death, from Greek mythology to the rituals of the Druids—marked the corner of the churchyard. An eerie photograph from that day captured Maureen's father walking her through the cemetery to the church entrance, a lush bouquet of rosebuds and lilies of the valley flowing from her hands.

After the wedding, they honeymooned in Paris and then flew across the ocean to begin their life together in Connecticut. They set up a comfortable apartment in a house with a porch on a tree-lined street. My father returned to Yale to complete his residency, and Maureen quickly found a position as a surgical nurse at the university hospital.

On a sunny July Saturday in 1960, they joined one of my father's colleagues for an afternoon boating expedition on the nearby Housatonic River. The river ran placidly, and they were enjoying themselves until the colleague, who was operating the boat, began to speed with abandon. Perhaps drinking was involved. Perhaps he was overeager to impress. Whatever the reason, without warning, he turned the boat hard, and Maureen, who had been hanging on tightly, was thrown overboard. The boat struck her; the propeller cut her chest. In an instant, said the coroner's report, she was dead of a traumatic head injury.

It took hours for divers to locate her body. My father paced the shoreline into the evening, willing her to be alive. He alone knew that, while they had been married for only four months, they were expecting their first child. The coroner's report would confirm this too.

These details were not revealed to me all at once. The day I discovered Maureen's picture, my mother simply told me her name, explained that she had been a nurse too, and that she had died in an accident. That was about all my third-grade self could handle.

A few years later, when my brother presented my parents with a pamphlet from his dream summer camp with a cover shot of a boy being pulled behind a speedboat on water skis, my father slammed his fist on the table and said that no child of his would be spending any amount of time near motorboats—period. Later, my mother would fill in the fuzzy details about what had happened on the river. When my father moved to New Jersey to begin his medical practice five years after Maureen's death, "Rumors were flying among us nurses at the hospital," my mother said. One particularly gruesome version involved Maureen's head being completely severed.

As a teenager, I came to know Maureen through the letters she and my father had exchanged, which I'd discovered neatly tucked into a shoebox in my parents' walk-in closet. Every time they were out for the evening, I settled on the floor with a flashlight and read through the handwritten notes, which were arranged by date and rubber-banded by year. It was a treasure trove of romantic love, a shared commitment to their work, and dreams for the future. I hoped I would be so deeply in love myself someday.

I would often emerge from the closet and whisper to my brothers something along the lines of, "Did you know none of us would be alive today if Maureen hadn't died?" The fact that someone had to die for us to be born was an existential conundrum that rattled our young brains.

Sometimes, when I was annoyed with my father, I'd stamp about loudly, wanting to let him know that a tragedy in his life did not give him a pass to yell at my brothers or to give me "the Look"—a terrifying, wrathful expression that had the effect of getting me to stop whatever I was doing without his need to utter a single word.

And sometimes, when I was annoyed with my mother, I pretended that Maureen had been my real mother. Mostly, though, I spent a lot of time wondering how my mother handled this beautiful woman's presence in her midst. A woman so lovely, so ageless, so perfect, that she and my father never had time for the luxury of an argument. When I was old enough to articulate this, my mother looked at me and said, "When someone you love is in pain, there's nothing you can't bear in order to help them." I would come to understand this later too.

When I was almost twice the age Maureen had been when she died, I was out on a walk with my father and finally worked up the nerve to ask the question that had been forming on my lips for years. What happened to his colleague, the man who had been operating the boat? Was he ever prosecuted? Did my father ever hear from him again? My father shook his head slowly. "No, he left school quickly and moved back south, where he was from, to avoid a legal action."

"Do you hate him?" I asked.

"Not anymore," he said.

Later still, I would come across the man's name on a law firm's billing statement, which my father had kept meticulously in a file, alongside his English marriage certificate and Maureen's death certificate. With trepidation, I took the paper over to the computer and entered the man's name into the search bar. Within seconds, I had found him. I found his medical CV (complete with abbreviated time at Yale) and the names of his spouse and children. I could see his estimated net worth. I could pull up images of the last two houses he owned. I pictured him playing in the yard with his grandchildren, as my father had liked to do with his.

I was haunted by the thought of calling his home number, which was listed too. What would I say? "My name is Barbara Becker. Becker. My name may sound familiar. . . . Please don't hang up—I'm not calling to upset you. It's just that I've thought of you a hundred times in my life. . . ."

I wanted desperately to tell him that my father had managed to go on. In many ways, he had thrived. He had married another nurse, my mother, whom he loved equally, if differently, he would say. He had three children, six grandchildren. Even after he stopped practicing medicine, the work he had done was a never-ending source of meaning. As my father's friend and former roommate Shep Nuland had written to me when we struck up an email correspondence over our mutual interest in death and life, *I seem always to get back to the same thing, which is that the prime elements in happiness are to have found one's work and to have loved.* My father, truly, had found both.

There were other things I yearned to tell this man. Unimaginable things happen. You can pull away from a dock as two and return as one. You learn that death is more than a single moment in time. Instead, it involves generations of people— parents, children, friends. Every one of the players will need to find their own way to navigate through what happened. You save money to donate a science lab in your late wife's memory, as my father did. Without telling anyone, you write a check each Christmas to have someone lay a wreath at your husband's late wife's grave, as my mother did. You fight to make a new law, as my father's lawyer did on his own time, forbidding those operating vessels with alleged negligence to escape prosecution by leaving the state. You learn to water ski anyhow, as both of my brothers did. You imagine conversations with people whom you would never really call in a million years, as I have.

I just need to know, what has your life looked like?

Do you still sometimes think about what happened that day?

Have you told your children?

Have you suffered?

How did this death change your life?

Maureen and her father in the churchyard
Buckinghamshire, England

My sister-in-law once innocently asked why I still think about Maureen as much as I do, even though her death was over fifty years ago.

Maureen's death and my life are entwined, I responded. When I encountered her, I felt I had no honest choice but to bear witness to what had happened. And to make sense of the ripples of this history that continue to spread out before me, just as ripples expand across a lake in autumn. A river in summer.

ANN

The first time I truly thought about my own mortality was while crouched low in the back seat of a van that was being threatened by a crowd wielding rocks and sticks.

It's not easy to explain what had brought me to the countryside of Bangladesh during a period of ideological and political instability. Rather, there was a confluence of reasons behind it, some more logical than others.

One had to do with falling hopelessly in love with a young man from New York City. I had met him on a New Jersey beach a few years earlier, after I witnessed him perform a simple act of kindness for someone I knew, who was having a tough day. Anyone who helped out my friend Jimmy, whose developmental disorder caused him to struggle sometimes, was destined to be my friend too. Quickly, though, we discovered there was more to it than a simple friendship. We shared the same values and interests. When our tastes differed, we thought they complemented each other well. Soon I was spending more time at his apartment on the Lower East Side than at my quirky, all-women's residence hall in Greenwich Village. I liked his family, he liked mine. Our families even liked each other. Everything pointed to a lifelong commitment full of happiness.

One morning, though, I awoke to find him sitting up in bed, wiping at his eyes. He had come to understand just how much he wanted a Jewish family someday, he explained quietly, and, while he knew I was religiously open-minded, he did not know if this could work for me. He explained that he was torn between his love for me and his commitment to his culture and his family, many of whom had not survived the Holocaust.

I was devastated by the thought of not being with him and needed some time to be by myself. Time to give us space while we thought about whether we could find a way to be together or whether this was truly the end. Going to the other side of the world for a while felt like a good option.

But the reason behind the reason that drew me to Bangladesh was my naïve idealism. By some stroke of fate, karma, or dumb luck, I had been born into a time and place of abundance. There was food on my table, health in my medical charts, and love in my family. I felt a sense of duty to share the riches that I had done precious little to earn.

Along the way, I had encountered others who were equally driven by a sense of justice and fairness. I enrolled in a graduate school for international studies and met many smart and ambitious students from around the world, many of whom had already been working to right the wrongs they had witnessed. A few of my classmates had lived in Bangladesh, studying with Muhammad Yunus, the founder of a well-known organization dedicated to poverty alleviation, who would later go on to win the Nobel Peace Prize. After I graduated, I too was on the lookout for a role model, one who took idealism and married it with pragmatism, who could hold on to both vision and hardheaded solutions. If my role model could be a woman, even better.

Through the connection of a close friend, I landed an internship in New York City working with an academic-turned-activist named Ann Dunham. Like Muhammad Yunus, Ann had devoted her career to alleviating poverty. For many years she had lived in Indonesia, where she became interested in the cottage-industry work that women did to support their families. Eventually, she became a pioneer in the field of microcredit, where the model is to distribute small loans to low-income borrowers in order to jump-start their businesses and help them gain economic empowerment.

Ann and I discovered a shared love of her field of expertise, anthropology, which had been my focus in college. She enjoyed collecting batik textiles as much as I enjoyed collecting masks— art that allowed people to express themselves through their cultures. Ann exuded a bohemian yet motherly wisdom around the office to me and the other women on staff and also in talking about her own children, of whom she was very proud—a daughter who was about to set off on a post-college backpacking trip through Mexico and the southwest United States, and a son who was a lawyer in Chicago.

Internships are often either monotonous times filing away a supervisor's paperwork or stepping-stones leading to exciting new opportunities. With Ann it was all about opportunity. The

United Nations was on the cusp of the Beijing World Conference on Women, a gathering of experts and world leaders that promised to set the global agenda for gender equality for years to come. Ann felt that microfinance was key, if only she could somehow demonstrate the benefits of lending small sums to poor women. This is where I came in, she explained.

"You've worked with video before," she said. I nodded, knowing that she and I both knew that my experience was limited to having edited a few low-budget videos for another non-profit organization. But she had an infectious way of believing in people.

"I want you to make a video in Bangladesh on microfinance that tells the story of poor women in their own words. We'll air it at the UN conference in China. No one wants to hear only about economic statistics. That would bore them to tears. *Show* us how it works, how women use profits to educate their children, seek out proper nutrition and health care for their families, fix the leaking roofs over their heads, become leaders. Everyone wins."

I could barely contain my enthusiasm. The project was everything I had been studying and working toward. It was an opportunity to dive into issues I cared about, to collaborate with a team of local women filmmakers, and to be creative and persuasive. And the timing was perfect, what with the need for some space from the boyfriend/not-boyfriend.

"Give it your best shot," Ann instructed, encircling me in her arms before I left her Midtown Manhattan office.

"Ann, I don't have words," I said.

"None are needed," she replied.

Everything started well. Upon the advice of my classmates who had lived in Bangladesh, I bought a couple of modest *shalwar kameez,* long-sleeve tunics and flowing trousers, in Queens, New York. I booked a room at a Dhaka guesthouse frequented by expats.

By the time I arrived in Bangladesh, the country was experiencing unrest. A doctor-turned-author named Taslima Nasrin had recently published a novel about tensions between Hindus and Muslims. Now Islamist leaders were demanding that Nasrin be put to death for her perceived criticism of their religion and her outspoken views on the need for a new order, one that would include the equality of women. Nasrin was in hiding, and there were an increasing number of threats against foreign organizations providing assistance to women and the poor.

Thus I found myself in the midst of a conflagration over issues I believed in but in a context I knew very little about. Where before there was only excitement for this opportunity, fear began to slip in.

One early evening I was in a van with two other foreigners—one from the Philippines and one from South Africa—along with three Bengalis. We were returning from a three-day visit to a village in the northern countryside. The trip had been exhilarating. I had watched women receive their first loans with tears in their eyes, while the more senior borrowers cheered them on. The women had found me peculiar. They leaned over my shoulder and watched me write in my notepad in a script that was unfamiliar. One asked our translator if I was sick—she had never seen someone with white skin and wondered if I might like to lie down. One night, the bank branch manager's family killed a chicken and presented the cooked meal to us proudly. I hadn't eaten meat in a few years but didn't want to insult them, so I did my best to swallow a few pieces. In the evenings, the women turned a wooden table in the office into a comfortable bed with a few light blankets, and I slept amazingly well.

We hadn't been on the road for more than an hour on our trip back to the capital when we saw ahead a blockade of burning tires and thick black smoke. A group of men twenty-strong had gathered and more were coming, many carrying sticks and bricks. Our driver muttered something in Bengali that had to be either a curse or a prayer. I had read about but never before seen a *hartal,* a planned strike that shut down businesses and transportation. These political skirmishes had been happening with frequency across the country, and some bystanders, I knew, had been injured or lost their lives. Coming from the village, we had assumed the demonstration would be over and that it would be safe to be on the road again. Now, with a crowd forming quickly around our van, there was no turning back.

My mouth went dry as I reached up to make sure my blond hair was completely covered by my brown *dupatta* scarf. I lowered my face and sank down in my seat, tucking my video camera between my feet.

Several men approached and looked menacingly into the van's windows. Their eyes seemed to be lit by an internal fire of rage, and they began pounding at the glass. Suddenly the door behind me was yanked open. I could hear a man yell, "America! America!" Maybe he had seen my blond braid, but there was no way he could have known I was an American. I threw myself onto the floor of the van, trying to stay out of their reach.

Now the driver's-side door was being forced open. A man from the crowd pushed our driver to the middle seat and took control of the steering wheel, speeding off with us. What was going on? Were we being hijacked? What would happen to us? I was the only woman—what would happen to me?

Everything seemed to be unfolding in slow motion, as if I could see each moment frame by frame. I watched the temple of the Filipino man in front of me pulsing over and over again as he clenched and unclenched his jaw. I heard an exchange of heated words between the Bengali passengers and the driver, which seemed impossibly clear but made no sense to me whatsoever.

As we sped out of the limits of the town, I noticed the sun setting to my right, an enormous pink sphere over an impossibly green field. A feeling of calm came over me. I imagined someone arriving at my parents' house in New Jersey to tell them I had died. I wanted to comfort them, to let them know that the end hadn't been all bad, that I'd managed to find a moment of peace.

I have no idea how far or how long we had driven when, in a completely wordless communication, the three men in the row of seats in front of me, along with our original driver, seemed to make a collective, instant decision. The man behind the hijacker stood, leaned forward, and opened the driver's-side door as we were moving. The other men pushed him out the door, and our driver slid back over to regain control of the van. The landscape was a blur as we sped in the direction of Dhaka.

No one spoke. Minutes passed. Finally, I said one of the only words I knew in Bengali: *dhanyabad,* thank you. No response. "That was close," I said, trying again, needing to release the adrenaline surging through my body. Again, my words were met with silence. I didn't know if the stoicism was cultural or gender-related. It was as if nothing had happened.

I left Bangladesh a month later, the finished video in my canvas carry-on. In spite of that incident, there was much I loved about the country. I would remember the *adhan,* the call to prayer, amplified through crackling speakers atop the minarets of Dhaka's old mosques five times each day. The hospitality of my colleagues who welcomed me into their homes for trays of cardamom-topped sweets. And the rural areas where women in colorful saris would place their babies in my arms, sharing their most prized possessions for a few minutes while barely disguising their wish that a spinster in her twenties like me would hurry up and start a family. Even before I stepped onto the plane bound for home, these experiences, along with the unexplainable moment of peace I had found in the midst of the attack, gave me conviction that sitting on the sidelines of life was not an option. I wanted to drink in human connection and revel in the ways in which we are different yet fundamentally alike.

Shortly after I returned to New York, Ann Dunham, only fifty-two years old, was diagnosed with terminal cancer after being misdiagnosed and treated for appendicitis. She didn't make it to the screening of our video, which received positive attention from the delegates in Beijing. I never had the opportunity to speak with her again, and I felt the emptiness of our unfinished relationship.

As she lay dying in the hospital, I later learned, her daughter rushed to her bedside. She read a story to her mother from a book of folktales in which a human transforms into a bird who then takes flight. She told her mother that, like the bird, she too could take leave. Fifteen minutes later, Ann was gone. I felt a welling of tears when I heard that story and hoped that, when the time came, I could have that kind of presence of mind for my own parents.

Years later I would see a photo of Ann in the newspaper with her arms wrapped lovingly around a young black boy. The child, it turned out, was her son—who would one day go on to become the President of the United States.

Visiting women borrowers of the Grameen Bank in Bangladesh

I think of Ann often and with deep gratitude—not only for being a role model but also for unknowingly helping me solve the boyfriend issue by giving me an excuse for the space we needed.

I had come home to find said boyfriend waiting at the airport with a bouquet of sunflowers, my favorite. Together, we enrolled in an intensive course for non-Jews looking for a greater understanding of Judaism and for Jews seeking a deeper connection to their heritage and traditions. We read the Torah, visited a different synagogue every week, and learned to recite prayers over cups of wine and challah bread that we had braided by hand.

With time, I accepted into my heart the dream of our some-day having a Jewish family. He accepted that my sense of meaning in life was more likely to come from many places rather than just one. A few years later, we stood on a mountaintop, under a *chuppah,* or wedding canopy, made from the prayer shawl that had once belonged to his grandfather. Before our families and friends, we vowed to be with each other, through all life would bring, until we, like Ann, would become as birds, ready to take flight.

ARDEN AND ADELE

Aspen, Colorado. I had really wanted to love this town, and for a moment, I did.

Dave and I had been married for two years when I joined him there for a work conference held at a resort, the kind of place with enormous stone fireplaces and chandeliers fashioned from elk antlers. Snow glistened on the majestic peaks, and the town was bustling with a Nordic-themed festival complete with snow sculptures and fireworks. I breathed in the crisp air and could practically hear John Denver singing "Rocky Mountain High."

The first months of pregnancy had been pure elation, and I was sure I'd done everything right. I begged off skiing with our good friends from New York City, Gary and Chris, who were also in town, and opted for a slow walk along a river trail lined with white-barked aspen trees. At a cocktail reception held in an art gallery, I asked for seltzer with a twist of lemon. Afterward, I skipped the cedar hot tub and climbed into bed early with Dave.

After a year of infertility treatment, I began to feel like a mother the moment I learned I was pregnant. Gone were the early mornings sitting anxiously in the crowded clinic waiting room, feeling like nothing more than a last name/first name/ date of birth. Often now I noticed myself humming softly to the tiny being growing inside me. I was in awe of the miracle of life, how a microscopic union of Dave's and my DNA could morph day by day to become the person who would make us a little family of three. In the evenings, we would try out names for either a girl or a boy, opting for short names to go with Dave's long last name.

We were waiting until we returned from Aspen, for the final doctor's visit of the first trimester, before telling anyone we were expecting. Not even Gary and Chris knew, though Chris raised an eyebrow and smiled when I stealthily tried to swallow a huge prenatal vitamin with my orange juice at breakfast.

Back in New York City on a Monday morning, I knew something wasn't right when the ultrasound technician, who had moments earlier been asking about our trip, suddenly stopped talking. Her face wore a blank expression as she scanned the monitor.

"What are you seeing?" I asked, terrified.

"Wait for a minute while I get the doctor," she said without meeting my eyes. When the door closed, I immediately reached for my phone to call Dave. "Something's wrong," I said, tears already beginning to flow down my cheeks.

A few minutes later, the doctor was in the room in his white lab coat. "Good morning," he mumbled, becoming the second in what felt like a long line of people who would not look at me directly. I watched him carefully as he pulled on latex gloves, adjusted the ultrasound wand, then leaned in closer to the screen to get a better look.

The heartbeat, which had been so steady and strong in past exams, was now gone.

Two days later, Dave and I were at an outpatient surgical center for a D&C. My eyes were swollen from crying, and the only comfort there seemed to be was Dave's warm hand holding my freezing one.

Earlier we had been arguing about whether to tell people about the miscarriage. Dave said yes. I said it was complicated. We hadn't let anyone in on the pregnancy itself, let alone the backstory of infertility, and all of it felt too exhausting and too raw to share. The very act of seeking treatment had already proven that my body just couldn't do what it was designed to do, I told him. Even as I said it, I knew I'd never let a friend get away with a statement like that.

"And what if they blame me for doing something wrong, like flying to Aspen?" I asked. An unshakable feeling of guilt had lodged itself in my gut.

"No one we know would be that insensitive," he replied.

In the days before podcasts and blogging, before Facebook was even a twinkle in Mark Zuckerberg's eye, I had literally never heard nor read a single firsthand account of infertility or miscarriage. I'd never felt so alone.

I watched a needle enter my arm and felt only mildly sedated as the nurse placed my feet in the stirrups and spread my legs wide. The instruments on the stainless-steel tray in front of me looked like the tools of a medieval torture chamber, I thought in a panicky haze. Dave put his forehead on my shoulder and whispered, "We'll try again. No matter what happens, it will all be okay."

That night, I propped myself up against the pillows on our bed at home and called my parents. My mother answered. "Can you put Dad on too?" I asked.

"Hi, Annie," my father said cheerfully. "To what do we owe the pleasure of this call?" he asked.

I started crying before the words even came out. "I had a miscarriage," I blurted.

There was a brief pause, and then my mother said softly, "I'm sorry," the three syllables I had been willing someone to say.

My father was silent for a long moment. Finally, he said, "Annie, this too shall pass."

A week later, two pieces of mail arrived. One was the medical lab report from the D&C. I opened the envelope before taking off my coat. The tissue sample had revealed no genetic disorder. I couldn't tell if this should make me feel better or worse. I also learned the gender, something I had specifically asked the doctor's office not to tell me, for fear of becoming more attached than I already had been. If the pregnancy had survived, we would have had a girl.

The other envelope contained a note from my father. Reserved in speech but expansive in writing, my father would, I knew, send a letter that would offer something for me to consider. I poured a glass of water and sat down on the couch. His handwriting was stereotypical of a doctor's, nearly impossible to decipher. I squinted and read . . .

> *I thought I would share with you a hard-earned insight that has come to me over the years. Maureen's death remains to this day for me a largely personal matter. I made my own accommodation to it. I thought that to share it, or to seek consolation, would have diminished my personal capacity to go on. Now I believe that solace is found both within ourselves and among others. You will find your own way of making peace with your loss, I am certain.*
>
> *Love,*
> *Dad*

Up until that point in life, I realized, I had never developed any coping skills for times when life got difficult. I didn't have to, because, for the most part, nothing had ever really gone wrong. And if I did happen to meet a challenge, I dealt with it by just trying harder. Grades? Put my nose to the grindstone. Job? Double down on networking. Relationships? Fight the tendency to want to be alone and put myself out there more. I was determined, obstinate even. It worked every time.

This longing for a child, though, was entirely outside the realm of trying harder. My body flat out refused to obey our dreams, no matter how earnest they were. The stress was so unmanageable that I noticed an ever-present quivering in my limbs that would sometimes cause my teeth to chatter, even on the warmest days. When I read about a scientific study documenting that struggling with infertility produces the same levels of anxiety and depression as being diagnosed with cancer, I was only a little surprised.

But my father's letter had left an impression. *You will find your own way of making peace with your loss.*

What happened next I can only describe through the benefit of hindsight, for only now can I see that I was taking an intentional step into the darkness, trusting I'd eventually find some sort of light to see by. Somehow, rather than running from my pain, I chose to stop and face it directly by signing up for a silent meditation retreat.

Perhaps it wasn't that far-fetched an idea. After college I had lived in Japan, where I had a job teaching English not far from the famous temples of Kyoto. On my weekends off, I would occasionally wander the grounds, marveling at the meticulously raked rock gardens where gravel flowed like ripples of water. My American roommate was studying Zen and asked me a few times if I'd like to join her to meditate. But at twenty-two, I could think of hundreds of things I'd rather do than stare at a blank wall for hours.

Now, when an acquaintance mentioned that he had just

returned from a meditation retreat in rural Massachusetts, something clicked. I made up my mind in an instant. I was going.

It took less than a day to realize that there's not much silence at a silent retreat. While I, along with my fellow meditators, took a vow of outward silence, the ever-present self-talk inside my head formed a deafening cacophony of senseless random voices.

Did my college boyfriend become a ski instructor as he had planned? Wow—my mom used to make sandwiches out of green bread for St. Patrick's Day. Where did she get that idea? Where is the nearest B&B? Can I get there without a car if this becomes too much?

On the second day, I signed up for a five-minute interview with a teacher. "How's it going for you?" she asked as I sat down in a chair opposite hers in a little room near the main meditation hall.

More than a little embarrassed, I explained the contents of my wildly scattered mind. She smiled. "That's totally normal," she said. "And it's an important first step—noticing the stories our minds spin, constantly luring us out of the present moment." She paused. "But mindfulness is not only about intentionally noticing your thoughts and feelings come and go, you know."

"What else is it, then?"

"It's about noticing them without judgment." *Without judgment.* I took that in. Was it even possible to let the thoughts and emotions simply be without getting lost in them, without beating myself up?

The teacher's steady gaze felt disarming. "Try that for a while," she said, standing to let me know the interview was over.

Once again I took my seat in the large hall and wrapped my shawl around my shoulders. Thoughts started seeping in again, darker this time. The story of my miscarriage began to play out. . . . The technician avoiding eye contact. The dehumanizing procedure to, as they called it, "empty the contents." And afterward, my body, tricked by the remaining pregnancy hormones, overcome by waves of nausea and morning sickness, with absolutely nothing to show for it. Every moment felt like it had been recorded and was playing back in high resolution with surround sound.

On my meditation cushion, I watched myself caught in dangerous, coursing rapids. "Notice *this* moment, without judgment," I repeated to myself, trying not to sound harsh as I braced my hands on the sides of the cushion as if it were a canoe headed for the edge of a waterfall.

I tried again, seeing thoughts arise like overhanging tree limbs, treacherous boulders, and spinning eddies. "Watching blame now," I said to myself, labeling feeling after feeling as I got pulled along with the current. "Watching sadness." Occasionally I would find myself in a pool of still water and take a breath.

The more I kept at it in the hours and days that followed, the more I felt like I could sometimes see the landscape as a bird could, soaring high above. There was no denying the close-up reality that Dave and I had lost the pregnancy we wanted desperately. Equally true was this newer view occasionally coming into focus—a certain kind of perspective that was wide enough to include both the pain and the possibility of being kind to my hurting self.

At the end of the retreat, a woman named Janet offered me a ride from Massachusetts back to New York. I was eager to talk to another meditator about her experience. It was pouring rain, and the dirt parking lot had been transformed into a bed of quicksand. When we dragged our suitcases through the puddles to her car, we found one of her tires completely flat.

"I'm really sorry," she said. I was eager to get home to Dave, but I was on a post-retreat high. "That's okay," I said truthfully as we waited for the local garage to send someone.

We sat inside her car and swapped stories of sore knees and necks. She asked me what had brought me to the retreat, and I surprised myself by telling her about the miscarriage. "Had you chosen a name?" she asked. Dave and I had never told anyone the name we had picked.

"Arden," I said in a near whisper.

"That's beautiful," she replied.

"Thanks. We named her after the place where we were married, outside of New York City, the Arden House. Also there's a

Forest of Arden in a Shakespeare play. I liked the name as soon as I heard it."

An hour later we pulled out of the retreat center, riding slowly on a flimsy spare tire. Janet put her hazards on as cars and trucks zipped past us. As she drove, she told me about her life.

"My husband and I divorced after being together for thirty-five years," she said, turning up the speed of the windshield wipers. "There I was, sixty years old and having to support myself for the first time. I hadn't been in the workforce for decades," she said, shaking her head. "So I got a job doing the only thing the local agency had available—cleaning bathrooms at a nursing home."

"What was that like?" I asked, relieved at Janet's lack of need for small talk.

"I'd been at Buddhism for a while, and I'd read a bunch of books by Thích Nhất Hạnh," she said, referring to the famous Vietnamese Buddhist monk. "He said, *Washing the dishes is like bathing a baby Buddha. The profane is the sacred.* So I took that on. Me—a woman who at one time hired someone else to clean my own bathrooms! But I scrubbed those toilets with pure attention," she laughed. "Toilet after toilet, day after day. Buddhist practice is like that. We learn to simply do what's in front of us without the whole drama." She laughed again, then added, "It surely doesn't mean that I didn't apply for other jobs as they became available."

We sat in silence for a while, as I watched the slick expanse of highway before us. After a while, she turned to look at me. *"No mud, no lotus,"* she said, quoting Thích Nhất Hạnh again. "Out of the muck of life, beauty will emerge."

When I returned home, I discovered I was pregnant. I had been pregnant the whole retreat, without even knowing it.

Our son Evan came screaming and kicking his way into the world a year after Arden would have been born. Two years after Evan's birth, Dave and I would lose a second pregnancy, another girl, who we had wanted to name Adele, after my grandmother. Once again, the pain washed in, but this time, the experience had a different quality. For the first time, I was willing to see that what was happening wasn't so much a roadblock keeping me from life—it *was* my life. It wasn't at all what I had wished for, but it was mine to work with, to make sense of.

Learning to meditate reminded me of summer vacations at the beach with my father when I was a child. My father was never more relaxed, more available, than when he was at the shore. I remember him teaching me to dive under approaching waves that seemed to dwarf my small body. "No matter how big they are," he advised, "there's always a calm place under the waves, near the sandy bottom." And he was right. In contact with the ocean floor, I could feel the gentle tug of the currents in my long hair and hear the otherworldly crackling around me, knowing that I was safe.

Evan (right) and Drew

Nearly five years after we lost Arden, I gave birth to a second boy, Drew, delivered in distress with the umbilical cord wrapped tightly around his neck, but healthy and wildly intent on living.

Arden, Evan, Adele, Drew—a braid of interwoven strands running through the life of my little nuclear family. I think about the girls sometimes, even as I watch the boys kick a forbidden soccer ball in the apartment or find the pot they used to cook macaroni and cheese, unwashed and perfectly messy in the kitchen sink.

Many years after we lost Arden and Adele, I spontaneously posted on Facebook:

Let's just try something here. Today, October 15, has been designated as a day of remembrance for pregnancy loss and infant death, which includes, but is not limited to, miscarriage, stillbirth, SIDS, the death of a newborn. To show how many of us are in this boat together, please consider leaving a comment . . .

In the first comment, I left Arden and Adele's names. I had never before breathed their names publicly.

I was blown away by the response. Nearly one hundred came forth, women and men, telling one another of their losses. While I considered all of them my friends, I had known about less than half of their experiences. My heart broke open, appreciative of the vulnerability and honesty of this community. Maybe we were all tired of the silence. Maybe we wanted our loved ones to be seen, finally. Perhaps social media provided just the right distance to be safe. Whatever it was, it was beautiful and brave, and I knew that when it came to grief, silence was no longer an option for me.

CONSOLEE

One bright morning on the cusp of autumn, I was pushing Evan in a stroller to his daycare in Lower Manhattan. I preferred the half-hour walk from home over the crush of the subway commute. I was running late that day for my job at a women's rights organization, located nearby on Wall Street. I was about to push the stroller into the crosswalk in front of the iconic Woolworth Building when I heard a thunderous noise. It sounded like an enormous truck hitting a heavy, metal construction plate at top speed on one of Manhattan's patched-together streets. I abruptly lifted my head to scan the roadway.

A few blocks away, black smoke was pouring out of the North Tower of the World Trade Center.

There must be universal body language for shock, for I and every person around me instinctively froze, our hands covering our open mouths as we stared up at the unfolding horror.

An unsettling thought came over me as the smoke increased and debris started falling: People inside could be facing their deaths right now. It was a sickening and surreal realization. Remembering suddenly that I had a nineteen-month-old child in the stroller, I angled it so Evan couldn't see what was happening. It was too late. He barely had words at that age, but he furrowed his little brow and exclaimed, "Fire! Fire, Mama! Fire!" as he pointed his tiny index finger toward the building engulfed in a ball of flame. It was a word and gesture that he would repeat over and over again in the months that followed, an endless replay that shredded my nerves.

I ran with the stroller against the forming crowd, turning around only once to get another look. That's when I saw a passenger airplane, flying improbably low, slam into the second tower.

Manhattan was postapocalyptic in the days and weeks after 9/11. With the bridges and tunnels closed to all but emergency vehicles, we felt cut off from the rest of the world. Armored National Guard trucks rolled down the streets of the Lower East Side on their way to what had become a smoldering mass graveyard. I tried to keep the windows closed against the acrid smoke, but somehow the smell managed to seep in through the cracks anyhow.

The Internet was down and phone service was sporadic, isolating us even further. In the parks, family members and friends began posting photos of missing loved ones. Dave spent hours each day at the Victim Information Center in Greenwich Village, checking for any news about the missing husband of a friend of a friend. There was hardly ever an update to the lists, and Dave slowly realized that this husband and father of three young children was in all likelihood dead.

Once I was able to return to work, there were several copycat bomb threats in our office building, forcing the evacuation of every floor. The receptionist was hospitalized for asthma aggravated by the ongoing thick dust. Worst of all, one of my colleagues had lost her brother-in-law, a father of two the same age as Dave, who had reported to his job at Cantor Fitzgerald on the 105th floor of the tower that day and never returned.

None of us were getting any work done. Grief counselors were brought in; as we sat around the conference room table, they encouraged us to share our stories of what had happened. Of what was still happening. A somber-looking counselor said, "It's critical that you find a way to work on this now. If you bury your trauma, it is guaranteed to come back to you, even years later when you are not expecting it. One death has the power to activate all of the losses you've ever experienced."

I swallowed hard and told the group about something I knew I had already stuffed down deep—that one of the pieces of falling debris I had seen when the tower was hit hadn't been debris at all. It had been a human being, jumping.

I began to question the job that I had once viewed as a dream job. I loved the people I worked with. I loved the president of the organization, who had allowed me and two other moms on staff to start an on-site infant-care center for the babies until they were one year old. I loved my sunny office, which had a commanding view of the East River. I loved working on women's rights. But up the road, thousands of people had lost their lives. Was I doing enough for the world, writing press releases, keeping up a website? I felt that I was in an ivory tower, disconnected from the problems people were facing on the ground.

I had known intellectually that life could be unpredictable, but now there was no denying the reality. If death and trauma could happen at any moment, on such a large scale, how, then, should I live? And what was my responsibility to others who experienced catastrophes around the globe?

A few months later, I resigned from my job so I could begin working with activists living in places that the world often forgot. Within another few months, I received an offer to consult with an organization that gave an award to human rights defenders, all of whom had risked their lives at the hands of brutal regimes. Standing up to injustice, they had been imprisoned, tortured, raped, kidnapped. There was a young man in hiding who secretly recorded and exposed the brutalities of the militant Islamic State in Syria with his cell phone; a student activist who spent years in solitary confinement for leading a peaceful pro-democracy campaign in Burma; a Korean minister who personally guided dozens of refugees out of North Korea to freedom via an "underground railway." One journalist from Russia with an indomitable spirit would later be assassinated in the elevator of her apartment building, a year after I worked with her.

Many steps removed from the day-to-day dangers they faced, I did the best I could to help them tell their stories to a global audience and to advocate for change. It was through them that I learned the meaning of courage. I had known that such people existed—Mahatma Gandhi, the Reverend Dr. Martin Luther

King Jr., Mother Teresa—but they had always been distant figures, somehow superhuman. It turns out there were many more than I thought. And now I was meeting them face-to-face.

Sitting across the table from these activists, inviting them for a meal to meet my family, waiting on a subway platform together for a delayed train, I began to notice a couple of things about them. They were realists, not minimizing the abuse they had endured but intent on refusing to allow it to rule their lives. They had strong ties to caring friends and colleagues whom they could call any time of the day or night. They also seemed to share a heightened sense of perspective that was at once vast and narrow. They could articulate that their lives were meant to be lived in service to something far greater than themselves, be it a principle or a belief. Yet so many of them also seemed to be able to zoom in with a magnified appreciation for simple things. Sweet plantains fried just right, or a child's silly joke told with perfect imperfection. *To see a World in a Grain of Sand / And a Heaven in a Wild Flower,* wrote the poet William Blake, who had met many social change activists of his time. Every time I came across those words, I thought of those I was meeting.

Consolee Nishimwe was one of these activists—a survivor of the genocide against the Tutsis in Rwanda—who quickly turned into a friend after I met her at a commemoration of the atrocity. She was fourteen when the brutality came to her hometown. Her father was the first to be viciously murdered. Then her three little brothers, ages nine, seven, and sixteen months old, were killed, their bodies thrown into their septic tank while the crowd chanted, "Hutu power! Hutu power!" Their names always struck me as beautiful, so worthy of repeating—Philbert, Pascal, Bon-Fils. Four days later, Consolee was tortured and raped by a sword-wielding neighbor—a man who had once been a friend to her family. She learned afterward that she had contracted HIV.

To know this story was to know only a small piece of Consolee's life. In addition to her work speaking and writing about the horrors of genocide, she became an advocate for others living with HIV. I was awed by her quiet confidence and the delight she frequently found in everyday life. This delight expressed itself in an enormous smile revealing a space between her two front teeth—a mark of great beauty in her culture.

Well-being had not come overnight; it took years. For half a decade, Consolee cried herself to sleep at night, overcome by feelings of shame and loss. Gradually, with the support of other survivors, as well as professionals who helped her to achieve physical and mental stability, she started telling herself that no matter what hell she went through, past or future, she could still have hope if she still had life. Instead of dwelling on pain, she said, prayer and meditation were key for healing and guidance.

One September morning, fourteen years after 9/11, Consolee and I were both in Central Park to catch a glimpse of the new pope, Francis, who was on a visit to New York City. Along with eighty thousand other people, we had won lottery tickets to watch his motorcade pass by.

I had been curious about this man who defied convention, who insisted upon living in the Vatican's relatively modest guest-house rather than the palatial quarters of past popes. A man who opted to visit prisoners and eat with the homeless rather than schedule time with politicians and the business elite.

As the crowd waited, I checked my phone. Consolee, who was several blocks north of me in the park, had posted a video of a rainbow she'd just spotted above the crowd. In the audio I could hear her saying in her melodic accent, "Wow, a rainbow! What an amazing sign." The day had been dry, with bright-blue skies and a few wispy clouds.

When Consolee's video went viral that day, many people commented that the appearance of the rainbow was like a miracle, an auspicious moment. Others were critical, saying a rainbow is in no way a sign or miracle—it's purely a scientific occurrence, caused by sunlight and atmospheric conditions. But if the world sends the unbearable our way, even in the form of genocides or terrorist attacks, what harm could come from seeking out uplifting symbols that remind us of possibility? It was like the T-shirt I once spotted in the window of an East Village shop: *There are only two ways to live your life. One is as though nothing is a miracle. The other is as though everything is.*

Thanks to the gift of working side by side with human rights champions like Consolee, I too am learning to pause and notice the simple things—even as the years continue to be

Consolee in New York City
(Photograph by Christian Kayiteshonga)

marked by the memories of 9/11. Every year on the anniversary, I ride my bicycle downtown to the firehouse next to my old office. I stop at the makeshift altar outside honoring the fourteen first responders who were willing to run in the direction of tragedy—even as I, hands gripped tightly on stroller handles, ran in the opposite direction.

And every spring, I stop again, this time in wonder, as an abundance of daffodils bloom across the city. After the attacks, a Dutch bulb supplier, heartbroken for New York, sent a gift of one million daffodil bulbs, which arrived by ship in the New York Harbor, one of the first vessels to enter after the port reopened. With millions more planted since, the city's hillsides, schoolyards, and humble sidewalk tree pits are transformed into life-affirming blankets of yellow, the color of remembrance.

When our city, nearly two decades later, would find itself under lockdown during the Covid-19 pandemic, the daffodils once again were welcome companions during my walks through deserted streets. It's like a rebirth every year, and with them, my heart opens a bit more to the possibility that hope can take root, even from the ashes of unfathomable loss.

Call it what you will—even a miracle if you'd like.

MAC

The islands of the Caribbean are alive with pirate lore, where merchant ships once plied the waters with cargo of molasses and kegs of rum. So maybe I shouldn't have been surprised when a pirate, well over six feet tall with ruddy skin and wind-blown hair, came strolling down the beach in my direction.

As I had been on high alert scanning the horizon for the menacing wild donkeys that sometimes make their way down narrow trails of vegetation to rifle through tourists' picnic baskets, I saw him coming long before he arrived. I nudged Dave's sand-covered toes with mine, and he looked up from his pile of trade magazines, which he swore he'd toss by the end of the day. I nodded my head sideways in the pirate's direction.

The pirate was hardly a terrifying Blackbeard. In his turquoise-blue swim trunks, he seemed to be a mainlander on vacation, just like us.

He stopped at our encampment of colorful towels, beach toys, and bottles of sunscreen and smiled. The boys, now shaded in his shadow, glanced up from their castle and moat construction.

"Good day, young mateys," he declared, hands on his hips, smiling at them. "Methinks ye may be interested in some real buried treasure," he said with a thick pirate accent that sounded vaguely Bostonian. "I noticed an X marking the spot right over yonder and thought ye might try digging there." He looked at Dave and me and winked.

As if a sign that prayers are answered, our six-year-old buccaneer and his three-year-old deckhand jumped up and ran off with their blue and green shovels in hand, in the direction he had pointed. Dave and I stood to greet him.

"I'm Mac." He was clearly having trouble dropping the pirate accent. "I hail from Glosta, Mass. And those five are my first mates." He indicated an area of beach towels where five kids, ranging in age from eleven to twenty-three, were spread out, some napping, some sitting up and playing cards. The youngest, a boy, looked at us and waved.

Dave shook Mac's hand. "I'm Dave, and this is Barbara."

I shook his hand and added, "And the boys are Evan and Drew. We're from New York City."

None of us could tell you exactly what the boys found hidden in the sand that day. Maybe it was some spare change from Mac's pocket or a couple of braided friendship bracelets or a pair of dice donated by his children. But it doesn't matter—the treasure they found (or that found them) that bright island morning was Mac himself.

Over the next five days, Captain Mac, as he came to be called by all of us, found a home in our hearts. We were spending the winter holidays in the same tent community, a campsite built into hills covered in dense vegetation, where ancient iguanas stared down from their perches in the trees. Not so charming were the absence of hot water and the enormous brown bugs that crawled out from the cracks between the wooden boards of the platform and into our tent at night.

We ate each evening at the communal dining pavilion over-looking the bay and the islands beyond. The day after we first met Mac, he came over to our table at dinnertime with a bowl full of butter pats and a couple of forks.

"Yo-ho-ho, mateys," he announced. "Methinks yer not tak-ing a fancy to those baked potatoes." The boys started chuckling. "Argh! Baked potatoes! How about we make mashers instead?" He pulled up a seat, handed each boy a fork, and demonstrated how it was done.

The next night, *Pirates of the Caribbean* was showing on a screen rigged from the rafters of the pavilion. The boys were asleep in our arms, but Evan woke up when the pirates were transformed into skeletons on a moonlit night. It took ten sec-onds for him to go from horrified to bawling. "There, there, matey," Mac said, reaching his hand over Dave's plastic chair to rub Evan's arm. "These things are merely a figment of the imag-ination! And I should know, as a pirate and all."

Mac's kids were lively and fun-loving. They mainly stuck to-gether, showing up for the camp's evening activities in a huddle. On New Year's Eve, the girls wore shimmering summer dresses and the older boys looked rugged and handsome. They showered their youngest brother with attention and took turns swinging him around to the tunes of "La Bamba" and "Oye Como Va."

"What made you decide to come here, Captain Mac?" Dave asked as the music switched to the calypso tune "Day-O." For the first time I could remember since meeting him, he dropped the pirate accent. He looked at Dave with an eyebrow slightly raised and said, "Well, my wife, Annie, died of breast cancer two months ago. She loved to sail these waters when she was a young woman. So I decided that coming here was just what my kids and I needed."

My lungs slackened like sails on a windless day. "Oh, Mac, I'm so sorry," I stammered.

"In the end, all that really matters is your family and love. The river of love . . . Annie had always said we should drink from it," he said, looking out over the treetops. "She would have loved our new mateys. They've brought us good cheer."

I couldn't get Mac out of my mind. I made a mental checklist for facing loss, things I was learning from him. *Gather your loved ones near. Get away, preferably into nature. Be generous with your time and imagination.* I craved answers for the living, for those of us who remain.

On the last morning of our trip, we brought our packed duffel bags to the pavilion to meet the shuttle, a rickety pickup truck retrofitted with open-air benches in the back. We walked over to Mac's table and hugged him and his kids. Drew offered Mac's youngest a green plastic dinosaur from his Bob the Builder backpack. Mac bent down to tousle the boys' hair. "Take care of your parents," he instructed.

"I don't have a pen or paper on me," he said. "But if you're ever near Gloucester, call the Chamber of Commerce. Everyone there knows how to find me."

Three days after we got home, I sat at my desk overlooking our neighborhood's red-brick buildings under a looming gray sky. I was wearing two layers of sweaters and a hat because our heater refused to turn on. I picked up the phone and dialed the Gloucester Chamber of Commerce.

"I'm hoping you can help," I told the receptionist. "I'm trying to get the address for a Mac in Gloucester."

"Oh yes!" the receptionist said brightly before I could even find his last name. "Hang on one minute, and I'll get it for you."

I reached for a pen and wrote his address directly onto the envelope that held a card with an aerial view of New York City. After hanging up, I wrote inside, *From the riverfronts of Manhattan to the shorelines of Massachusetts, your pirate lads and their parents are missing you.* I thanked him for the gift of his presence and told him how moved Dave and I were by his kindness and resilience. I put the letter in the mailbox across the street, feeling sad that one of life's little chapters had come to an end so quickly.

A month of school, dinners, sports, and activities passed. I was again at my desk at home when the doorbell rang. I opened it to find Patrick the UPS man with a large box on his handcart.

"This one is addressed to the kids," he said. I noticed that the return address said Gloucester.

That night, the boys sat on the family room floor and tore the package open with their little hands. A note at the top said: *Ahoy, mateys! Didn't want you to think I'd forgotten about you! Be good! Captain Mac.*

Inside were separately wrapped trinkets containing pirate tattoos, eye patches, skull rings, and an illustrated book about a salty pirate whose heart softens after a pauper named Sandpiper finds his glass eye. There was a Jolly Roger flag, a bag of plastic pieces of eight, and an album of songs about shipwrecks, whaler men, and pirates, accompanied by penny whistles and a fiddle.

At the bottom of the box was a gift with an envelope addressed to Dave and me. Inside was a card with a quote by the poet Hafiz on the cover: *There are so many gifts still unopened from your birthday; there are so many handcrafted presents that have been sent to you by God.*

"You open it," I said to Dave, my eyes stinging.

Dave smiled and pulled the gift out of the tissue paper. He handed me the ceramic bas-relief picture frame with a painted pirate and a treasure chest. The photo inside was of Mac, his kids, and a woman who could only be Annie, wearing the telltale headscarf of a person undergoing chemo. Her thin hand was holding Mac's tightly, and her other arm reached around one of her daughters.

Put in a picture of you 4 cuties and leave us tucked in back, Mac had written in the card. Dave passed the frame to each of the boys, who studied all of the faces. Then he got up and put their picture on the windowsill, right alongside the many photos we have of our families.

For four years we exchanged holiday cards. Then, when Evan was ten and Drew was seven, we took a family trip to Maine. I studied our guidebook to New England to see how far off the route we would be if we stopped in Gloucester to see Mac on our way home. "Gloucester is America's oldest seaport," I read aloud. "Her fishing fleets were in danger of invading pirates and enemy warships during the War of 1812. Cannons were set up on the hills to protect them."

"Real pirates!" called out Drew from the back seat. "I knew it was true!"

"I don't know, Dave," I said. "Maybe he's moved on. Maybe we should just leave this as a happy memory."

"Are you kidding?" Dave responded. "If you don't call him now, I will."

I dialed his number from my cell phone. "You're only thirty minutes from here," Mac said excitedly. "Bring the mateys by!"

A half hour later, we drove our dusty wagon crammed with camping gear and piles of dirty laundry onto Mac's gravel driveway. His home sat on a wide expanse of lawn overlooking a rocky point and the bay beyond. He came out of the house, greeting us with wide-open arms. "Look at you," he said. "You've finally made it."

He offered us seats on the brick patio and brought out lemonade. The kids went running across the lawn to swing in the hammock, Mac's dog following at their heels. "Be careful," I called out, remembering how my childhood friend Marisa and I had swung my brother too high in a hammock in her family's backyard and he'd tumbled out, breaking his collarbone.

Three of his children joined us. One daughter was home from studying in Rome while working for the United Nations Food and Agriculture Organization. His second-oldest son was involved in a sustainable-agriculture project in Gloucester. And his youngest was now a high school student, handsome and as friendly as his father. The conversation turned to Annie.

"Annie had an incredibly adventurous spirit," Mac said. "She lived in Florence the year of the catastrophic flooding. She sailed across the Atlantic with her father, hitchhiked across the country and into Mexico during college, waitressed at Durgin-Park—where she got fired after her first day because she was called 'too sweet' for the notorious historic Boston eatery—and was an assistant teacher in rural, not-yet-integrated South Carolina. She was even a taxi driver in Boston for a day." Dave was especially intrigued by the last, as he had a license to drive a New York City bicycle taxi, which he did purely for fun on weekends and evenings while holding down his day job.

"Our kind of woman," I said, as his kids got up to join ours in exploring a beach hut at the water's edge.

"Over a thousand people came to her memorial service right here on the lawn, the same rainy day the Red Sox celebrated their first World Series victory in eighty-six years," Mac said. "That win was what got our little guy through." He swept his arm toward the house. "Annie died in the same room here where she gave birth to him—eleven years to the day and hour in the same room where her mom had died."

"What got you through, Mac?" I needed to know.

"You know that song 'Don't Worry, Be Happy'?" he asked. "The expression came from an Indian spiritual teacher Annie and I followed named Meher Baba. 'Death isn't really the end,' he'd say. 'It's only the end of this body.'"

As the sun began to slip behind the trees to the west, Dave and I got up to leave. Mac called over to the boys, who came running up the lawn. "I checked with the kids, and we wanted to know if you'd like to have their collection of Legos." The boys were jumping up and down when Mac and his boys carried four huge plastic bins full of Legos to the driveway. We looked at our overstuffed car. Drew, sensing a dilemma, offered to sit on top of a bin instead of in his booster seat.

"We'll make this work," Dave said, popping open the lid of a bin and pouring the Legos into the footwells of the back seat. As we drove off, the boys turned around and waved to Mac until long after he was out of sight.

That night in our hotel room outside Boston, I looked up Meher Baba online. "Listen to this, Dave," I whispered, so the kids wouldn't wake up in the double bed next to us. *"If death has any value, it is to teach the individual the true art of life. . . .*

A true aspirant neither seeks death nor fears it. And when death comes to him, he converts it into a stepping-stone to the higher life."

"That explains what he meant by 'death isn't really the end,'" Dave whispered back sleepily.

I continued reading to myself. Meher Baba's brother Jamshed had died a young death, of which he said, *You at times travel in a train, and other passengers, without a care in the world, depart at different stations . . . all according to their tickets. In the same way, Jamshed was traveling, and when he reached his destination, according to his ticket, he departed from the train—left his body. His station was nearby. But according to you, he has passed away in his youth. The trains go on running day and night, and numberless passengers travel in them, and depart at different stations according to their tickets. How many are you going to weep over?*

It felt soothing but foreign to think that the amount of time we have on earth is predetermined somehow. It took away the second-guessing about when it was going to end, because it was already written, so to speak. A done deal. If that were the case, the only thing left to do would be to fully inhabit the time we have now. Try your best. *Don't worry, be happy.*

The next morning we woke up early and dropped Dave off at Boston's South Station so he could catch a train back to New York. I rearranged the Lego bins in the vacant passenger seat to make more room for the boys in the back. Without the time pressure of needing to get Dave to work, I could make a stop at a place I had always wanted to visit, Walden Pond.

When I was growing up, my mother's guidebook to life had been the Bible. My father had many guidebooks, but near the top of his list was Henry David Thoreau's *Walden*. Beginning in 1845, Thoreau spent two years, two months, and two days in a one-room cabin he built with his own hands on the shores of the pond. Like many of Thoreau's readers, my father admired him for his resistance to slavery, his disdain of materialism, his deep love of nature, and his keen observations of the world around him. I admired these qualities as well. But there was something else that drew me to Thoreau. He felt like a kindred spirit when it came to thinking of death and life as inextricably intertwined.

To my reading, Thoreau's experiment in simple living was really about a profound desire to live fully in the face of mortality. Three years before Thoreau moved to Walden Pond, his brother, John, whom he revered, had cut himself while shaving and later died of tetanus in Thoreau's arms. *I went to the woods because I wished to live deliberately, to front only the essential facts of life, and see if I could not learn what it had to teach, and not, when I came to die, discover that I had not lived,* he wrote, in what became the essential statement of the book.

"It's just a half hour away," I told the boys, getting behind the steering wheel.

"Oh, Mom," Drew groaned. "Do we have to go there?"

"We'll get pickles and black-and-white milkshakes on the way home," I bribed, remembering that Mac had told me about

Rein's, a traditional Jewish-style deli they stopped at on trips between Gloucester and New York. "Look out for the sign they have that says, *Where Harry Should Have Met Sally,*" he had advised.

A short drive later, I turned off the highway and followed signs to the Walden Pond Visitor Center. We walked from the parking lot over to the public beach, where long-distance swimmers in wetsuits plunged into the water to train for their next triathlons. The mist coming off the lake into the cool air made it look like an ethereal cloud, hovering just above the surface. I could see why Thoreau had called Walden Pond a "lower heaven."

We set off on a trail alongside the pond leading to the original site of Thoreau's cabin. "Find a little rock to put there," I instructed the boys, picking up a stone on the path. Visitors have been adding rocks to a cairn marking the site of the original cabin since 1872, ten years after Thoreau's death.

Drew was filling the pockets of his shorts with fistfuls of pebbles, but Evan was grumbling and dragging his feet. The trees on the pond path were a mix of pine and deciduous, and it seemed to me that the green leaves were starting their subtle fade to fall.

"I don't feel good," Evan said, coming alongside me.

"It's just a little farther, Bug," I coaxed.

"Mom," he said again, and then threw up right in the middle of the path. He looked startled and then started crying.

"That's disgusting, Evan," Drew said.

I fished some napkins out of my waist pouch and cleaned his face, seating him on a rock. Then I scooped together a pile of soft pine needles and covered the vomit. Realizing my quest would go no farther than this, I put my stone like a gravestone on the little pile in the path.

"I'm sorry," Evan apologized as I held his hand and led him back to the car. I stopped and hugged him.

"That's okay, Evan, we didn't want to see that stinky place anyhow," Drew said.

Back on the interstate, resigned to my shortchanged pilgrimage, I thought again about what Thoreau's experiment in the woods had taught him about living in the face of dying. I knew he had died at the age of forty-four of tuberculosis aggravated by a trip to count the rings of tree stumps on a cold, wet evening. I pictured him stooping down to distinguish heartwood from sapwood, his finger sliding over each ring with quiet determination.

As Thoreau's body began to fail, his friends were alarmed by his diminished appearance yet amazed by his tranquil acceptance of death. "Never saw a man dying with so much pleasure and peace," remarked one visitor, who had been his jailer when Thoreau refused to pay a poll tax as an act of protest against the Mexican–American War. And when he was asked if he could sense the hereafter from where he lay, Thoreau responded, "One world at a time."

I glanced in the rearview mirror at the boys, who were now

Mac, Annie, and their children, Gloucester, Massachusetts
(Photograph by Freddy Purdy)

sound asleep, their heads bending toward each other. At moments like this, I too loved life, in all of its simple expressions and ordinary inconveniences.

Dave and I still keep in touch with Mac. He sold the house where his youngest son was born and where both Annie and her mother died, eventually falling in love with the architect who designed the new, smaller home he envisioned for himself. The last time Dave and I visited Gloucester, Mac and his girlfriend cooked a lavish dinner and insisted we stay the night. We sat in the candlelight, reminiscing about the idyllic campsite in the

Caribbean where we had met, which, now sold and converted to private property, can only be accessed through our memories. As we lingered over glasses of wine, Dave went out to the car and returned with the bins of Legos, long outgrown by our boys and ready to be loved anew by Mac's first grandchild.

CHRIS

One warm Saturday morning, around the time Evan was starting middle school, I took him and his friend Jack to an outdoor science fair in Queens. They learned how to solder blinking LED lights to a battery and make batches of a gooey substance called *oobleck* out of cornstarch and water. Afterward, we all licked at soft-serve ice cream cones while they told me about their favorite and least favorite teachers and guessed at who each other's secret crushes might be. Then they took off laughing, racing to a nearby fountain in the adjacent park and back.

That afternoon, tired and a little sticky, we boarded the #7 train, bound for home. Three men with guitars and wearing matching sombreros entered our car and started singing mariachi songs for tips. I was tapping my foot and clapping my hand against the metal subway pole when Evan nudged me in the arm and said, "Mom, your phone is ringing in your purse."

I answered, seeing Dave's name come up on caller ID. I faced the door and looked out the window at the view of the Citi Field baseball stadium from the elevated tracks.

I could barely hear him over the band. "I'm on my way to the hospital," he said in a steady voice full of strained effort. ". . . had a heart attack, and they don't think she'll make it."

"*Who* had a heart attack?" I asked loudly over the music. "I can't hear you." Several people turned to look at me.

"Chris."

"Chris? Gary-and-Chris Chris?" I asked in disbelief. Gary and Chris were the friends who had been with us in Aspen when I was pregnant with Arden. Always up for adventure, they had just returned from a trip to Great Britain with Chris's mother, Cathy.

But this news didn't add up. Chris was only fifty-four years old.

"Yes," Dave confirmed. "Chris." In the background, I could hear him closing the door to our apartment in a rush.

"My God," I said. Evan and Jack looked at me with worried expressions. I tried to make a brave face. "I'll drop off the boys and be at the hospital in thirty minutes," I said, looking at my watch.

When the elevator door opened onto the cardiac unit of Beth Israel Hospital in Manhattan, Dave was standing there to meet me. He wrapped his arms tightly around my shoulders.

"Two hours ago she was at the gym," he said, his voice cracking. "She was supposed to meet Gary for brunch after, but she called him from the cab to tell him she didn't feel well. And that was it. She passed out and the cab driver called 911. She's just come out of emergency surgery."

I wanted to anchor myself to that spot with Dave forever, as if not walking any further onto the unit would cause the whole nightmare to dissolve.

Dave led me to a seating area near a window overlooking the brick wall of an adjacent hospital building. Gary was standing in the corner, trying to reach Cathy in Texas. I went over and placed my hand on his arm, and he put his hand over mine. It was moist and cold. I noticed a sign that said IN USE on the door to a small family room across from us. The door was ajar, and several people were crying inside. This floor was bad news.

A doctor in green scrubs with a stethoscope around his neck approached us. He seemed to be about thirty years old. Gary put his phone down and looked at him.

"She lost a lot of oxygen to the brain before surgery," the doctor said, averting his gaze. I could see small beads of sweat on his temple. "Do you know if she signed a living will?"

I reached for Dave's hand as Gary followed the doctor into Chris's room, trying to imagine Chris now, when all I knew was her distinctive *joie de vivre*. In our house Chris and Gary were legendary for taking the boys trick-or-treating and on outings to the movies and bowling alleys, spoiling them with popcorn and cotton candy every step of the way.

After a few minutes, Gary came back to the window and sank heavily into a plastic chair. "The doctor said that if she comes out of this, she will never be the same." His voice was flat. "You can go in, if you want. She's not responding at all, though."

Dave and I walked side by side into Chris's room. A tangle of tubes and wires came from her limbs and chest, and a ventilator was breathing for her.

"Chris," Dave said, approaching the bed first. "It's Dave." He leaned over the railing, putting his mouth near her ear. "I *know* you can do this. We're all right here pulling for you." From the foot of the bed, I could see that she had recently painted her toenails an iridescent pink.

I willed myself to get closer. In spite of all of the machinery beeping and glowing around her, Chris looked peaceful. Her long golden hair and skin still tanned from summer made it appear that she was lying on a poolside recliner. What I wanted to tell her was different than Dave's message.

"Chris," I said as Dave stepped back and made room for me by the head of the bed. "You've fought as hard as you could. If you want to keep fighting, we'll fight with you. But if this is too much, you can let go when you're ready. I know you're worried about Gary. But he's like a brother to Dave. I promise you we'll make sure he's okay. And your mom too. We all love Cathy, and we'll look out for her."

I glanced at Chris's hands and remembered when she had proudly shown off her ring after their wedding in Savannah. Everything felt surreal. I leaned even closer to her ear so she could hear me over the rush of the ventilator. "I love you, Chris. Thank you for being our friend."

I know she heard me. Or at least I like to think she did.

I left the cardiac-care unit several hours later to be with the boys, longing to bathe in their energy, to hold them in my arms. As I passed by a room down the hall from Chris's, near the elevators, I glanced inside and saw a gaunt elderly man in a flimsy hospital gown sitting alone in an armchair facing the door. His eyes were wide with terror and he looked at me imploringly. His mouth seemed to form a single, silent word I could not make out. I paused for a moment, letting the scene fully register, and then turned my head and continued walking.

After Chris died in the early hours of the following morning, I wanted to be alone. I took a long walk along the East River near our apartment, feeling with each step that I was gasping for air. As I looked out across the water, an idea entered my mind. I stopped and in that moment made a vow to myself—that I would find a way to volunteer with the dying. The expression on the old man's face was seared into my brain, and I was so disappointed with myself for walking past him. It hadn't been my job to fix things for him, and there was no question that I was distraught over having just said goodbye to Chris when his eyes and mine locked. Still, I longed for a do-over. To pause at his door and to offer some sign that I had heard him. Or to go back to the nurse's station to find someone who could tend to his needs.

Was a do-over even possible? Maybe not in my relationship to that one man but in how I dealt with suffering in a wider sense? In the weeks and months that followed Chris's death, the memory of the stranger's face seemed to blend with the faces of my parents. I couldn't let go of the realization that they had far less time to live than they had already been alive. With both near eighty, this should have been obvious to me. Somehow, though, I felt stunned and saddened—as if for the first time—by the recognition that they wouldn't be alive forever.

Yes, I would need to find my way to be with the dying. It felt like Chris's final invitation to me.

My mother shook her head in disbelief and glanced at my father when I first told them of my plan to be trained as a hospice volunteer. She asked in a sweet but sincere voice, "How are you going to manage that?"

With years of nursing under her belt, she had good reason to question my decision. When I was in high school, she and my father had persuaded me to work as a candy striper at the local hospital, where they had met and fallen in love. Medicine was in the family, they reasoned, between themselves and my father's parents, who had been another nurse/doctor duo. Perhaps by osmosis or wishful thinking, I would be good at it too.

On my first day on the job as a candy striper, the volunteer coordinator had taken me to the pediatrics unit. I was wearing a pink-and-white-striped dress and matching cap, which my mother had helped fasten to my braided hair with bobby pins. With my uniform and engraved plastic name tag, I felt older and somehow official.

"Each year we sponsor a child from overseas so they can come here for reconstructive surgery," the coordinator said, standing at the door of one room. "This little fellow was born with a rare facial deformity. The sound you hear is from the tracheostomy tube that goes through an opening in his windpipe."

A soft gurgling came from the crib. The air around me suddenly felt heavy and hot, and I leaned against the doorframe for support. I never actually saw the child, because my vision faded to black, and I melted like wax to the floor. When I regained consciousness, a nurse was paging my father, who was on duty that day, to report to my side.

In tears that evening, I pleaded with my parents to let me quit. Seeing my distress, they reluctantly agreed not to push me into medicine.

Less than a year after Chris died, I was accepted into a nine-month program led by two Zen Buddhist monks who founded a center to train people in compassionate end-of-life care. A few of my classmates were doctors and nurses, but most of us were people who had been around loss and wanted to learn to live in greater harmony with it.

I had been meditating on and off since my miscarriages. The more I learned about Buddhism, the more relevant to real life it felt. The Buddha had begun his spiritual quest as a young and sheltered prince who snuck out of his father's palace under cover of night and was instantly confronted by scenes of old age, sickness, and death. *This will happen to me too,* he thought, *and to everyone else, be they kings or paupers.* His purpose became to find a way to experience inner freedom, even in the face of the uncontrollable human conditions that sweep through the lives of us all. I couldn't think of teachers I'd rather be learning from than those who had knowledge of the path out of suffering that the Buddha had uncovered through much sacrifice, hard work, and deep insight. I half-expected that studying with these two Zen monks would be like finding some kind of cosmic shortcut.

True to the Zen practice of vowing to be of service to all beings without exception, the teachers assigned me to work with patients in a twenty-five-bed hospice unit at New York City's largest public hospital. On the first day of class, I was busy taking notes, trying to absorb as much as possible before I met my first patients. There were some basic hospital protocols to be followed, like washing our hands between patient rooms and filling out a standard report after each visit. But for the most part, what was being asked of us was to show up with undistracted presence for every person we would encounter.

"The dumber you are in this work, the better," laughed Koshin Paley Ellison, one of the monks, who was sitting on a black cushion in a sparse, sun-drenched meditation hall in the Chelsea neighborhood of Manhattan. The younger of the two and a native of Syracuse, New York, Koshin had a shiny shaved head and a bright smile.

In a pattern I would come to recognize between them, the other monk, Chodo, added the next thought. "Start from

Chris in Liverpool, weeks before she died

a place of beginner's mind, approaching each interaction as something fresh and new." Chodo had begun life as Robert Campbell, growing up in Birmingham, England. With a salt-and-pepper beard and a slight British accent, he exuded a kind of confidence that felt at once straightforward and warm.

"Say the person in the bed wants to tell you about his favorite sports team," Koshin continued, picking up the thread. "Even if you couldn't care less about baseball, begin with a sense of genuine curiosity. 'Tell me what you like about the Mets,' you might ask. When you listen like this, when you put aside all of your preconceptions about the person before you, they will let you into their lives, their passions, and their struggles. Your time with them will become both a giving and a receiving, a moment-by-moment dance with life."

I found myself lured by their poetic way of saying the most mundane things. At the same time, I was scared of what I was about to do, intentionally putting myself in such proximity to death. The task of showing up and responding to what was needed in real time sounded too simple to be true. How would I face the sights, smells, and sounds that had literally floored me the last time I volunteered in a hospital? More daunting still was knowing that, week after week, I would be forcing myself to acknowledge that my parents and others I love would someday no longer be with me.

"Death will wake you up," Chodo had promised. I desperately wanted stay in bed, curl into the fetal position, and pull the blankets over my head. But Chris's death had taught me that the stakes were too high to allow myself to fall back to sleep. Everything depended upon being awake.

MRS. B, ROOM #724

The nurse at the front desk on the hospice floor had tipped me off that Mrs. B in room #724 could use a visit. She was in the final stages of congestive heart failure and didn't have much time.

It was my first week on the job as a hospice volunteer, and I was consumed by getting to know the ropes. I was relieved that the unit, with its white carpeting and abstract paintings on the walls, looked more like a tasteful boutique hotel than a place where people went to die. My biggest fear was entering the room of a new patient and figuring out how to begin. Koshin had advised us to simply say hello and find a chair. He always made things seem easy.

I knocked on Mrs. B's door and entered. Just beyond the large window near her bed, the East River shimmered in the early-morning light. Mrs. B was tenderly petting a stuffed animal, a bright-green tree frog that was resting on her legs, facing her with its large, unblinking eyes.

"Come in," she said. I noticed a rosary with blue beads and a silver cross in her fragile, aged hand.

"I'm Barbara, and I'm a volunteer here. Would you like a visitor?"

"Please sit down," she said, indicating the upholstered guest chair beside her bed. I was glad to be asked.

We chatted about the framed photos on her windowsill— her two daughters and many grandchildren. Recently there were great-grandchildren. She grew silent.

"What were you thinking about when I walked in?" I asked, sensing that she was waiting to see if I would accompany her to the truest place this conversation could go. It didn't take long.

"I know I'm not going to be around for much longer. Myself, I'm at peace with that. But Thanksgiving is a few months away, and Christmas right after that. I don't want to leave my family during the holidays."

I fumbled my way along with Mrs. B, acknowledging her sadness. I tried my best to leave the door open for the possibility that her daughters and their families would pick up where she had left off, carrying on the family's rituals, remembering her, and cherishing one another. Sometimes in loss, we remember most to love, I said.

Now a tear was following the path of a wrinkle etched into her face. I handed her a tissue from the bedside table, which she took with a shaking hand. "My grandson in New Mexico called yesterday. He's sad because he's not going to make it to see me before I pass, what with his job and all."

"Have you thought about writing him a letter?" I asked, seeing an opportunity to help them both.

She seemed to brighten a little. "I can't write anymore, but I can dictate if someone could write for me," she said, adjusting the clear oxygen tube that fit into her nose.

I walked with purpose down the hall to the volunteer office and after some searching found a stack of pretty pink stationery with a scalloped edge.

That morning Mrs. B dictated a letter to me for her grandson Keith. It wasn't long or poetic, but I knew she meant every word.

> *Dear Keith,*
>
> *I want you to know how much I love you. You have always been such a fine young man who has made me proud. I wish you all the best. I hope, if it's God's will, that someday you meet a young woman who you can start a family with. I will be looking down on you from heaven.*
>
> *I love you so much,*
Nanny

I added at the bottom: *Dictated to Barbara, a volunteer.*

After that, she asked me to write more letters—for her daughters, her other grandchildren, and even her great-grandchildren. She also had me write to her church community and her bridge club. *All of these people in her life's wide net,* I thought. *We should all be so lucky.*

When I was done, she asked me to put the letters in her

small overnight bag so that her family would find them easily after she was gone.

I wished I had some poetry or prayers memorized to recite at a time like this. But I could only remember the first line of a comforting Bible passage that had been made into a song. So I recited it:

> *To every thing there is a season,*
> *and a time to every purpose under heaven.*

"Thank you," she said, leaning her head back onto her pillow. "Do you have another?"

I recalled one that might fit. "Do you know the Serenity Prayer?" I asked.

"Oh yes," she said, smiling and seeming small, as if she were disappearing into her fluffy bathrobe.

God grant me the serenity to accept the things I cannot change—she was mouthing it along with me—*courage to change the things I can, and wisdom to know the difference.*

"I asked God to send me an angel this morning," she said. "Now I know it was you."

I asked Mrs. B if I could give her a kiss goodbye. Right there in room #724, I loved this woman called Nanny as if she were my own. I leaned over and brushed my lips against her warm forehead.

I have certainly never envisioned myself with wings of any

sort. We are, all of us, imperfect beings. But in that moment, I realized that we all carry a humble spark of connection and love, there for the taking and there for the giving, that simple gift of showing up.

THE ELDERS

Life was going along as usual. No insurmountable mountains to climb, no raging rivers to ford. It wasn't that we didn't have challenges. Dave and I both worked long hours, returning home each evening feeling spent but ready to jump into the next part of the day: dinner with the kids, paying bills, checking in with family and friends, and then collapsing into bed. *Show me parents who aren't exhausted,* I would tell myself, seeking solace in the low bar of modern life.

Eventually, everything changes, of course. For us, the run-of-the-mill life ended abruptly when, within the space of a few months, three of our elders, as we affectionately called our older relatives, were diagnosed with Alzheimer's disease. That's when we began to feel the full force of being members of the so-called sandwich generation: middle-aged adults caring for our children on one side and our elders on the other. One night while brushing my teeth, I snapped my toothbrush in half from the effort I seemed to be putting into everything.

In the assemblage of all disease, there was none I feared, dreaded, and despised more than Alzheimer's. Perhaps that came from having witnessed the decline of both of my grandmothers, who lived with us in my childhood home as their minds slowly unraveled. Perhaps it had its roots in hearing about an uncle who had been diagnosed with the disease in his early fifties. Perhaps it was that everyone in our household knew a little more than we cared to about the plaque and tangles that disrupted the healthy function of neurons. The brain was my father's profession, after all.

Now he was the first to be diagnosed.

My mother, brothers, and I had sensed the warning signs. His speech was becoming increasingly halting, and his spelling was wildly off. He had gotten lost driving to a nearby pool where he had been swimming for two decades. One day Evan led me to my father's desk to show me our family's holiday picture, upon which my father had labeled everyone by name so he could connect names to faces. I felt stricken.

The neurologist who made the clinical diagnosis was one of my father's hiking buddies. My mother said that after this friend and colleague delivered the news, she saw him turn his head away from my father and quietly wipe away a tear.

I stopped by my parents' house in New Jersey early one weekend morning for an unannounced visit. Neither of my parents ever complained about anything, so I thought I'd pop in unexpectedly to see if I could catch a glimpse of their unvarnished daily lives.

I found my father sitting in his chair at the kitchen table, reading the same article over and over again.

"What are you looking at, Dad?" I'd asked, leaning over his shoulder to get a better look. In bold letters across the top, the title read: *Diagnostic Guidelines and Disease Trajectory for Alzheimer's.* I stepped back, overwhelmed. My father, the retired neurosurgeon with the once-brilliant mind, was futilely trying to study the disease that was literally shrinking his own brain.

In our caregiving class, Koshin and Chodo reminded us often to use open-ended questions when talking to people experiencing a change in their health. But before I could formulate a good one for my father, I blurted out, "Dad! Isn't this a depressing thing to be reading about?"

He looked at me in astonishment and paused. "Oh no," he began tentatively. "There's nothing more fascinating to learn about right now." His eyes were bright behind his glasses smudged with fingerprints, and I knew then that he meant it sincerely. Feeling apologetic for my horrible leading question, I bent down to give him a kiss on his whiskered cheek.

We both looked up as my mom came into the room. I wasn't sure if he remembered her name any longer either. "As long as the lady of the house is taking care of me, things are very, very good," he said, and pointed in her direction.

My mother-in-law, Laura, was the next to be diagnosed. At eighty-three, Laura's body was in remarkably good shape. Her memory, though, was a different story. A few years earlier, we would have talked about the news headlines or the latest happenings at her job as a social worker for the elderly, a position she held until she was eighty. Now there were days when she was uncharacteristically confused and agitated.

One afternoon the boys were horsing around as usual, lobbing their stuffed animals at each other across the living room. "Boys!" Laura yelled. An unfamiliar look crossed her face, and she added mockingly, "How old are you? You should be ashamed, still having teddy bears at this age."

Evan looked at me and shrugged. Drew ran off to his bedroom and closed the door behind him. I found him lying facedown on his bed. "That was so mean," he said in a small voice muffled by his pillow.

I rubbed his back. "I'm so sorry that happened. It's not Grandma talking—it's this horrible disease."

I remembered the day I had tried to break through the firewall of my own grandmother's dementia. I had found her sitting in a chair in our family room, staring out the window into the woods, when I decided I was running out of time to ask her my burning questions about her mother, who had Native American ancestry. I knew it was a touchy subject because my grandmother had spent much of her life studiously assimilating. I wasn't expecting, though, the out-of-character fury my curiosity would unleash. My grandmother turned to look at me, fire flying from her dark eyes. "Stop!" she yelled, her voice quivering. I was shaken and felt a deep sorrow to have caused her pain. I was also crushed, knowing that there were truths about my family's story I would now never learn.

But for every bad day with my mother-in-law, there seemed

to be nine good ones. One Saturday morning in the spring, we met up with her and my father-in-law, Marvin, at one of our favorite green spots, a section of the New York Botanical Garden that contained an old-growth forest, the largest existing remnant of the original canopy that once covered New York City.

Laura was cheerful and childlike, twirling about in a new jacket that Marvin had bought for her. *"My ma gave me a nickel to buy a pickle, I didn't buy the pickle, I bought some chewin' gum,"* she called out, reciting a rhyme from her youth as she raced ahead. I turned around, hoping that the boys were catching some of this lighter side of Alzheimer's, but Drew was balancing himself on the top rail of the split-rail fence and Evan was furtively gathering pebbles for an imminent attack.

Laura stopped to face a robin redbreast that was taking a bath in the stream trickling alongside the trail, puffing its feathers and singing loudly. "Hi, little bird!" she exclaimed, and pursed her lips to whistle along. Farther up the trail, she paused to feel the smooth white bark of the birch trees. Her observations were so small and unexpected, and breathtakingly beautiful. Without her, I would have missed it all.

There's a Japanese practice called forest bathing, in which one slows down enough to see, hear, smell, and feel nature deeply, as a child would. Forest bathing—I liked the way that sounded, like the brain itself was being washed of all the pollutants that cause dementia. It reminded me of my father and his love of Thoreau, who spent four hours walking each morning. *An early morning walk is a blessing for the whole day,* Thoreau had written.

"Are you enjoying yourself too?" Laura asked. Her glasses were slightly crooked on her face, and her short gray hair was disheveled in the breeze. Her lips were parted in an open smile.

Yes, I too *was* happy in this moment, there in the woods, where even concepts as weighty as the cycle of life and death can make perfect sense. Mighty trees will fall, their trunks becoming fertile ground for new growth and life yet unseen. So it would be with our elders and all of the generations to come after them.

I asked Dave what he and Marvin had talked about while they stayed back, sitting on a weathered wooden bench at the start of the trail. Dave sighed. "He said he's been playing some old records for Mom, the classical music they listened to when they were courting. He told me that sometimes she'll sit on the couch crying over a Verdi opera."

Normally an image like that could draw me straight into melancholy . . . the tenderness of Marvin's gesture, and the remembrance of a time when he and his beloved could hold hands and let an aria wash over them, oblivious to a distant future that would someday be their load to carry. This was the heart of anticipatory grief, mourning a loved one before they're actually gone. Those feelings did not leave my mind, but there was something else too. After our day in the woods, I heard a faint but brighter tune that I simply couldn't name yet.

Around this time, I met a vibrant woman named Joan, who seemed to be in her sixties, with a head of curly hair and bright-blue eyes. She surprised me when she told me she was a Zen Buddhist monk.

"Tell me something about you," she asked sweetly. I could have said a dozen different things but startled myself by blurting out the story of my father and my mother-in-law and Alzheimer's.

Joan took both of my hands. "I'd like to give you a *koan*," she said, referring to the Zen practice of teachers giving their students short philosophical riddles designed to open their minds to a larger truth. I had never been given a *koan* before and was somewhat intimidated by what I knew of them. They seemed to be questions for which I'd never be able to give an adequate answer, try as I might. "What is your original face before you were born?" or "What is the sound of one hand clapping?" It seemed like it would take years to puzzle one all the way through.

I felt nervous, like a kid about to take a high-stakes exam, and wondered if my hands were perspiring in hers.

"I'm ready," I lied.

She looked intensely into my eyes and asked, "What is bigger than Alzheimer's?"

It hadn't even been a full week after receiving Joan's *koan* when another elder ran into trouble. This time it was my aunt Beverly, my father's only sibling. My brothers and I thought of Aunt Bev as a third parent. She was present at every holiday and family vacation we could remember, close enough to know the intricacies of our lives but distant enough to be able to offer sage advice without our taking offense.

Aunt Bev had been pushing the limit of her memory loss as far as it could go, living alone in an apartment in a quaint college town in upstate New York. She was an accomplished woman—a trailblazer when it came to women's equality in education and sports, a respected professor, the organizer of the first all-women ski patrol registered with the National Ski Patrol System, and a formidable visiting professor at West Point, where she was awarded the Department of the Army Outstanding Civilian Service Award. No one could convince Aunt Bev to move into an assisted-living facility, though we all strongly suggested it. One weekend, Dave and I had even driven to her place to take her on a tour of some tasteful senior housing nearby. "Not yet," she said firmly after seeing a hall full of walkers and wheelchairs outside the dining room.

I first knew something was seriously wrong with Aunt Bev when she told me weakly over the phone one day, "I'll be okay. I'll just make my way off the floor . . ." and then quickly backtracked. "I mean, I'll make my way to the kitchen and get a glass of water."

For the preceding three days, my mother, brothers, and I had been calling to check in on her.

On the first day of our phone calls, it sounded like Aunt Bev had strained a muscle in her lower back. She said she'd take some ibuprofen and would feel better in the morning. On the second day, it sounded like she was having a little trouble walking around the apartment. We made an appointment for her to see her doctor early the next week. And now on the third day, in bed nursing a bad cold myself, I called her after I took a nap. Aunt Bev sounded very small and far away.

"Do you need me to call 911?" I asked.

"No, no. It's not that bad," she answered faintly.

I told her to stay put and then called my brother. "David, she's on the floor. I'm going to call a friend of hers to go over there right now."

"I'm jumping in the car," David responded, grabbing his keys and leaving his family as they prepared dinner.

When David and her friend let themselves into Aunt Bev's apartment hours later, they found her in agony. She had no idea how long she had been lying on the floor beside her bed or how she had gotten there. David, with a few years of volunteer ambulance-corps experience under his belt, assessed the situation, carefully picked up her hundred-pound frame in his arms, carried her down the stairs of her walk-up building, and took her to the emergency room.

He called me two hours later. "None of what she said these past few days was accurate, Barb. Her pelvis is broken in four places, and she hasn't eaten or had anything to drink in days. We almost lost her."

I held it together until I hung up. Then I sat down at the kitchen table and put my head in my hands.

Two days later I took a train to Aunt Bev's town to relieve my brother and to take her by long-distance ambulance to a rehab center in New Jersey. At least there, someone in our family would be able to visit her every day.

When I arrived at her hospital bedside, I was surprised to see how small she looked compared to a month earlier, when I had visited and we had gone out to lunch. She knew my name but was in a delirious state, talking about my father, whom she always called Bud. It was as if they were kids again.

"Oh, a potato! How nice! I'll share it with Bud. He'll be so happy." Only there was no potato anywhere. I nodded along. It's much easier to enter their world than to contradict it with yours, as my mother had advised when my grandmothers lived with us.

"Aunt Bev," I said, "we think it would be better for you if you moved to New Jersey to be closer to Bud and to all of us."

"I'd like that an awful lot," she responded, smiling.

A few days later, I sat in the front seat of the ambulance as we rode past horse farms and onto the interstate. Aunt Bev lay sleeping on a stretcher in the back, next to an EMT who checked her vitals every twenty minutes. Our friend Gary texted to wish me a happy birthday. I had completely forgotten what day it was. After Chris died, he had taken on the task that had once been hers of reaching out to us for our birthdays. I texted back a heart and told him where I was. *Ask them to turn on the sirens for you,* he replied with a winking emoji.

What is bigger than Alzheimer's? Joan's question again entered my mind.

We're meant to ingest these *koans,* metabolize them, become them. *Switch from the thinking mind to the mind behind the mind,* I instructed myself, as if I had any clue what I was talking about. Out past the stigma of Alzheimer's, the fear and the suffering, out past separation and death, there had to be something else.

I felt like I might fall asleep and rested my head against the window, closing my eyes, the nights on Aunt Bev's couch finally catching up with me. In my mind's eye, I was sauntering through the woods with Laura once again. Nature was definitely bigger than Alzheimer's, I thought dreamily. My father's curiosity about the disease that was devouring his brain as he read his medical prognosis at the kitchen table—his tenacity was bigger than Alzheimer's. Half awake, half asleep, I envisioned my brothers, my mother, my husband, my kids, standing in a circle, surrounding Dad, Laura, and Aunt Bev. The care of one human being for another—even when one person may not recognize the other—is bigger than Alzheimer's, I thought. And what about love? Isn't love bigger than Alzheimer's?

My head bobbed, and I was alert again. I rubbed my neck.

"Getting some zzz's there, huh?" the driver asked.

"Maybe," I said, wondering if I had. Then I wondered if my response sounded rude, so I asked about the black ink lettering wrapping all around his forearm.

"What does your tattoo say?" I asked. He glanced over, as if trying to decide how honest he wanted to be.

"It's a couple of lines that have gotten me through a lot in life. Kind of like my motto. *Point me to the sky above. I can't get there on my own.*"

My father and Aunt Bev

"That sounds profound," I said. "Where does it come from?"

He looked at me again, a little shy this time. "From my favorite band, the Misfits."

"Nice," I said, nodding. I smiled as I watched the pine trees recede into the distance.

A daughter/daughter-in-law/niece pondering a Zen *koan,* and an ambulance driver guided by a punk-rock band. At the end of the day, does the source of our inspiration truly matter if it gets us where we need to go?

PRIYA, ROOM #714

In my first year volunteering on the hospice floor, there were certain rooms I tended to sidestep. If I saw that a patient was about my age, I could dream up a handful of seemingly well-reasoned excuses to resist a visit, barely admitting to myself that it felt a little too close to my own impermanence. I knew this wasn't a good thing. So I tried to be kinder toward my mortal self, coaxing her gently to enter where she was scared to go.

Like the morning I read on the floor census—the detailed list of patients occupying each bed—that the woman in room #714 was exactly one day younger than I. What had happened to her? What brought her to this bed? Did she have a husband and children too? How were they handling her illness? I stood outside her door and paid attention to my breathing for a moment before entering.

Her window shade was halfway drawn, and in the dim light, I saw that she had a visitor seated in a chair at the foot of the bed. I willed myself to stand a little taller and introduced myself to both of them.

"Good morning. My name is Barbara, and I'm a volunteer. Would you like a visitor?" My standard lines again.

As if I were some kind of distinguished guest, the man

in the chair rose to shake my hand and introduced himself warmly as Aarush, the husband of the patient, Priya. He appeared to be in his mid-forties and looked exhausted, as if he had spent the night sitting upright. Still, I was moved by his hospitality in this confined setting and encouraged him to sit and rest.

I looked at Priya and raised my hand in greeting. Her black hair was an inch in length, probably growing in after chemotherapy was stopped. In her lap was a ruled composition notebook in which she was writing with a red pen. She glanced up at me and returned my smile before going back to the open page. I took a quick look—it seemed that on every line, she was writing the same thing over and over again.

"In Hindu culture, we have a practice of writing the name of Lord Ram continuously. *Rama, Rama, Rama* in Sanskrit," Aarush explained. "It's a very powerful mantra that is helping her gain clarity and drive away any bad thoughts."

"Oh! I've heard of this," I replied, remembering how a college friend's father, also Hindu, once told me about devotees repeating sacred words either through chanting or in writing to focus one's mind on God. *Japa,* he said it was called. It was said that Gandhi himself often repeated the name of Lord Ram, and many believe that his last words after an assassin shot him point-blank were *Hé! Rama*—O God!

Aarush looked surprised. "Do you know India?"

I turned to look at Priya, not wanting to disturb her concentration, but her head was down and she appeared to be completely absorbed by her meditation. I sat in the empty leatherette seat next to his at the foot of the bed.

"I visited India two years ago with my husband and our children," I answered quietly. "Mumbai, Delhi, Kerala, and Varanasi."

"What did your children think of our country?" he asked, shifting a little closer to the edge of his seat, offering me his full attention.

I found this question nearly impossible to answer in any concise way. During the trip, I felt as if the boys were keeping a checklist at all times. Spicy curry, *bad;* buttered naan bread, *good.* Cows in streets, *amusing;* incessant traffic and honking, *unbearable.* Smearing each other with colorful clumps of paint during the festival *Holi—amazing!* Everywhere we went, Dave and I had tried to infuse them with our affection for the country but knew they would only see it through their own eyes.

So I told Aarush another story.

"The thing my boys will remember most of all is the little yellow cricket mallet they bought in the outdoor market in Varanasi. It was plastic and probably for toddlers learning the game."

Aarush nodded, encouraging me to go on.

"Every time my husband and I stopped to check our guidebook, the boys would start up a game wherever they could find a bit of space. Kids would appear from every direction to play with them. One morning they were playing along the Ganges and the ball kept rolling into the river. My husband waded in several times to fetch it."

Priya stopped writing. She looked up from the page and smiled.

"A dip in the Ganges is very auspicious indeed!" Aarush explained.

I thought of the last day in India, when Evan and Drew beckoned a boy to play with them. The boy, who had been begging on the street, kept shaking his head to decline, but our boys were persistent. I watched as more-affluent people made clucking sounds of disapproval, but Evan and Drew were oblivious to this and finally succeeded in convincing the boy to take the mallet and bat. The boy's smile lit up the entire street.

"How long have you been here?" I asked, wanting to connect beyond my travel experience. Priya lowered her head again and went back to the task at hand.

"We came three days ago in the middle of the night, when she was having pain. We left home so quickly that I didn't have time to bring any of her music or the objects from our altar. Our daughter won't be able to come from college in Chicago until this weekend."

A daughter. So Priya had a child a little older than Evan. The fact that Priya's life had begun just one day after mine arose again like a dull ache in my chest. A troubling calculation presented itself: Priya had hit "middle age" when she was in her twenties. I hoped she and her husband didn't notice me taking a slow, deep breath.

I was relieved when there was a knock at the door and the

doctor assigned to her came into the room with a bright-eyed resident-in-training.

"I am going to give you some privacy, but I will be back," I promised.

As I walked out of her room, I wondered if I could be helpful. I racked my brain, trying to remember what a Hindu altar looked like. In the volunteer office, I rooted around for something that would jog my memory. In a large box of supplies to use with patients—colorful pipe cleaners, glue and watercolors for arts and crafts, nail polish and manicure kits—I pulled out two battery-operated votive candles and flicked them on. That was a good start. Next, I picked up a portable CD player and perused the shelf of CDs, setting aside classical music and holiday tunes until I found a compilation of Hindu *kirtan* songs by the devotional musician Krishna Das. What luck.

Then I went in search of Mary, the volunteer who brought fresh flowers for the common spaces each Monday. I found her humming to herself at the supply room sink, cutting stems and filling vases with water. "There's a woman named Priya in #714 who could use a small bouquet," I told her. "I have plenty," Mary said cheerfully, arranging bright-red tulips in a porcelain vase and handing them to me.

Fifteen minutes later I was back in Priya's room with the makings of an altar. Her husband cleared a space on the windowsill and we arranged the sparse offerings. When I hit play and Krishna Das's voice came over the small CD player, Priya glanced up at me and smiled again.

"This is very, very good," her husband said as he stood back to admire our handiwork. He continued, "You should know that for us the music can be from any religion. In Hinduism, it is all one."

I laughed at my perfectionism. How often had I made the mistake of thinking I must read all the books on Hinduism—or any topic, for that matter—before I could be of any help? It turned out that there was nothing more I needed to turn this moment into a sacred one. Just like Aarush, exhausted but rising to shake my hand, or like Evan and Drew, persuading a boy from the streets to join them in a game of cricket, even the smallest of gestures offered from a willing heart has the power to be transformed into bounty.

As with almost all the patients on the floor, I never learned what happened to Priya. I find myself a bit more easeful about mortality, mine and hers, when I think of her single-minded devotion and wish that in her final moments, the name *Rama* was dancing on her tongue.

FELIX

Some families have figurative skeletons in their closet. My family happened to have a real one.

For one hundred years, we'd been handing down from generation to generation a skeleton we affectionately called Felix. Felix came into our lives through my grandfather, who, eager to become a doctor following the death of his grandmother during the 1918 Spanish flu pandemic, entered medical school and was issued a human skeleton to use as a study aid in a gross-anatomy seminar.

Felix's body had already been tidied up by the time my grandfather received him. Sinew had been stripped from the bone; his skull had been horizontally sawed so that the skull cap could be removed and studied; his jawbone was fitted with a spring to keep it from falling off; and a nice clean hole was drilled into the top of his head so that his bones, which had been wired together, could be hung from a stand.

After graduating, my grandfather established his medical practice during the depths of the Great Depression, and Felix, who was apparently never expected to be returned to the school, found a home in his office.

In 1954, my father completed medical school, following in his father's footsteps. Felix came faithfully along to my father's office, once again lending his presence as a teacher of sorts. Right up until his retirement, my father kept Felix's skull on his desk and rehearsed complicated brain surgeries with it before entering the operating room. While the top of the skull resembles a smooth tortoise shell, the lower section is a landscape of ridges and valleys. An empty cranium, without the presence of a pulsing human brain, is an invaluable three-dimensional tool, my father once told me.

It was my brother George who became the next in our family to graduate from medical school and to offer his home as a resting place for Felix. It seemed fitting because his wife was also a doctor, and his two daughters were interested in careers in medicine. It looked like whatever else the future might hold for him, Felix would certainly not be lacking in attention.

All was well and good for a while, until Felix started showing his age. With each passing year, his bones turned more brittle. His paper-thin temples were cracking; the tips of his fingers and toes shed bits of grainy dust. Even the rusting wires that held his bones together looked like they were disintegrating.

I sat at my parents' kitchen table one morning as my mother, father, and I tried to decide what to do with Felix. Evan and Drew bounded through for a snack on their way to play basketball on the neighbors' driveway. They were interested in our conversation. Like me, they couldn't remember a time without Felix in their lives. And, following their curiosity, Dave and I had made a point of talking to them openly about what happens to the body after death. On our family trip to Varanasi, India, we went out in a rowboat one morning on the Ganges River to watch the sunrise. Varanasi is considered a sacred place in the Hindu religion. If you die or are cremated there, you will be liberated from the cycle of death and rebirth. Funeral pyres were burning along the shore. Family members stood around the fires, wailing and crying, while mangy dogs picked through the remains of nearby pyres that were now smoldering ash. The boys had been unimpressed. They said they thought it would have been different—bodies on fire floating down the Ganges, à la the Vikings. Theirs was an unusual perspective for children to have on the matter of our corporeal affairs, and having Felix around the house only added to that.

When I was a child myself, I wouldn't have been surprised to be told that every home had a skeleton lying around. Sometimes, I would sit in my father's swiveling desk chair, wiggle Felix's few remaining teeth, and wonder what he had been like while he was alive. Did he have brothers and sisters? How sad they must have been when he died, I imagined.

As an adult, I'd later learn about the ancient Buddhist practice of meditating in charnel grounds, where dead bodies were left aboveground to decompose or to be devoured by vultures and other wild animals. Monks would observe the spectacle of dissolution in order to avoid becoming overly attached to the body and thereby come to recognize the essence of impermanence and clear-seeing. Buddhism encourages us to allow death to sit on our shoulder, to become intimate with it. It is said that a day that goes by without contemplating death is a day not fully lived.

But *how* does one do this? One practice that especially resonated with me as an adult was called the Nine Contemplations by Atisha, an eleventh-century Bengali Buddhist master. I printed out the list and kept a copy by my bedside table to consider each morning: *All of us will die sooner or later. Your life span is decreasing continuously. Death will come whether you are prepared or not. Your life span is not fixed. Death has many causes. Your body is fragile and vulnerable. Your loved ones cannot keep you from death. At the moment of your death, your material resources are of no use to you. And your own body cannot help you at the time of your death.*

What I did understand, thanks to Felix, was that right under my flesh, I too contained a skeleton, a common representation of death itself. In this way, we are living with a constant reminder of our mortality at the core of our own bodies. It seemed that there were just two choices: either embrace the wholeness—the interrelated yin-yang of life and death—or fight our own transient nature.

That morning at the kitchen table, it was my mother who had an idea we could all live with. "I know!" she announced excitedly. "Let's cremate Felix and put him under the holly tree with us when we die." She glanced over at my father, who was nodding his head, perhaps at the thought of the tree and our family tradition.

The holly tree looms large in our ongoing story. It sits at the edge of a small New Jersey lake where my grandparents once lived. Today my brother David and his family call the same plot of land home. My grandfather had accepted the tree as a form of barter for the treatment of a patient who had been unable to afford his medical bill during the Great Depression. Actually, it was two holly trees joined, for a male and female holly tree must be in close proximity for pollination to occur and create bright-red berries. My grandparents' cremated remains were buried under the tree, and both of my parents wanted theirs scattered in the same spot. Each year, snapping turtles lay their eggs in a shallow nest near the tree, perhaps finding protection from predators in the spiky leaves on the ground. It seemed like a suitable place for death and life to coexist.

Many people never get around to making decisions about what they'd like to have happen to their bodies when they die. Not so for my parents, who deserved an A+ for preparedness. They had signed copies of their living wills and durable powers of attorney for health care and had placed a note on their refrigerator to help paramedics find the documents easily in case of an emergency.

They had also stipulated a no-frills plan in which a funeral-home owner by the name of Jim would pick up their bodies, cremate them, and deliver the ashes by hand to my brother, along with ten copies of their notarized death certificates. Jim had cremated my mother's mother and two of my mother's brothers, and my parents trusted him. All told, this would cost less than most caskets. There was nothing sentimental about it, and that level of expedience made my parents happy. "Save what's left for the grandkids' education" was their attitude.

Now they wanted Felix to join them.

No go, said Jim, the cremator. You need paperwork before you can cremate someone, even an old skeleton—a birth certificate, a death certificate, a Social Security number. Considering the fact that Social Security wasn't established until after Felix was dead, the only choice was to hand him over to the county medical examiner's office.

Before we delivered Felix to the medical examiner, I spent a little time with the skeleton. I wrapped him in a soft blanket, one that we had used for Evan when he was a little boy. Holding his skull, I peered into Felix's eye sockets one last time. I felt like Hamlet, sitting there with a head in my hands. *Whatever has the nature to arise will also pass away,* the Buddha had often repeated in his teachings. It was said that some people, upon hearing those words, became instantly enlightened. *Nothing is exempt from change,* I thought, pulling my sweater tighter around me. *Not even me.*

Before sealing the box, I placed inside a handwritten note relating how important Felix had been to my family, practically begging the officials to take good care of him. As an afterthought, I included my email address.

Six months passed. Then one day an email appeared in my inbox. *Skeleton,* read the subject line.

It was from a teacher at a public high school.

Thank you for your incredible donation! "Felix" has been put back together! One of the physics teachers helped me find and connect bolts and rods to redo the leg attachments and find an attachment for the head.

He has already been used to teach my classes and will be used by the anatomy and physiology students and the forensics students for many years to come!

I read through some forensics she and her students had applied to the skeleton, based on growth plates, insertion points for muscles on the bones, size of the hip region and the area above his eyes, as well as signs of arthritic changes. Felix was indeed a male, a Caucasian, between thirty-five and forty when he died.

Attached to the email was a picture of twenty students standing around the table, hands folded, many with their heads bowed. I imagined the hush over the classroom.

I could have fallen out of my chair when I saw from the teacher's e-signature that she worked at the same high school that my brother George's girls attended. Somehow, it seemed, we were destined to remain in close proximity to Felix throughout the ages.

What do I want to have done with my body when I die? I began to wonder. Given all that Felix had done for my family over

*Felix with my grandfather and his sister,
1927, Ocean Grove, New Jersey*

four generations, it seemed like common decency to offer my body in return. I did some research. With well over 100,000 people waiting for a lifesaving organ transplant, it seemed like organ donation would be a helpful thing to do for others. University medical schools and scientific facilities also need human bodies and may accept them after the needed organs have been harvested. *Harvested*—it reminded me of bountiful crops and Thanksgiving.

One organization would plant a tree on the one-year

anniversary of the cadaver donation, in a national forest in Colorado that just so happened to be down the road from the Rocky Mountain town where Drew would study for a semester in high school. I imagined Drew returning to the area someday with his own family, knowing that one tree in the midst of thousands came about because of my body. The path of my remains, or at least the part I could control, began to become clearer.

I decided that a lock of my hair under the holly tree would be a good substitute for having cremains to scatter. That way, I too could join my family, and the snapping turtles, at the lake.

I included all of my wishes in a handwritten note, sealed it in an envelope, and put it on my refrigerator for safekeeping, just like my parents.

MR. R, ROOM #734

"I t would be helpful to us if you could spend some time with Mr. R in 734," the social worker on the hospice floor said as soon as I walked into the volunteer office one morning. There had been two deaths the night before, and everyone was extremely busy talking to the families, filling out paperwork, and preparing the rooms for those who would come next.

"Sure," I said, hanging up my coat. "What can you tell me about him?"

"He's a Muslim man, in his seventies, and completely alone."

I put on my volunteer badge, pulled my hair back from my face, and set off down the hall, trying to bring to mind the little I knew about Islam.

I recalled a day a few months earlier, when I had been overcome by nostalgia on the anniversary of my childhood friend Marisa's death. I had thought about her all that day and about the time I had spent living life with the end in mind. I'd remembered the bucket-list trip to Turkey that Dave and I took with the boys, ages six and nine. The night we had arrived in Istanbul, I led my jet-lagged family to a darkened hall to see the whirling dervishes of the poet Rumi's order of Sufism, the mystical dimension of Islam. One boy on either side of me, I felt their sleepy bodies grow heavy as they leaned against my shoulders. Dave had looked over and smiled softly. In the blur of the dervishes' long, spinning skirts and alluring music, I had felt that all was right with the world.

The memory of being completely absorbed by the dervishes' embodied act of devotion had made me wonder if there was a Sufi community in New York City. I was surprised to find one within walking distance of our apartment, not far from where I had stood on 9/11 with Evan in the stroller, watching as the twin towers were engulfed in flames.

I wasn't thinking at all about future hospice patients when I walked through the front door of the three-story Sufi center in Tribeca those few months before. I entered into a large open room, where plush sheepskin rugs were placed in a circle on a floor covered with thick red Persian carpets. Two dimly lit chandeliers hung from the ceiling, and green banners with golden Arabic calligraphy decorated the white-painted brick walls.

A woman with short hair and round glasses put her hand to her heart in greeting and introduced herself as Zhati. "Come sit by me, and I'll explain everything," she said graciously, pointing to a seat on a wooden bench, just outside the sheepskin circle.

A few dervishes leaned over to say hello. There was a couple—newlyweds from Pakistan—a woman originally from Istanbul, and a man from Harlem.

The room grew quiet as an elegant woman of about seventy

entered and sat down. Zhati told me that she was Shaykha Fariha, the first Western woman to be named as the spiritual guide of this Sufi order.

"We don't worry too much about formal religion here," Shaykha Fariha said, addressing the gathering. "This Sufi path is the mystical path of love. Of the divine union between the Lover and the Beloved, which is our true essence. And the *zikr* is our practice of remembering God."

A woman with a white prayer cap circulated through the group, tipping a bronze genie-like bottle into each of our out-stretched hands. I took a cue from those who went before, holding my hands to my nose to smell the rose water, then rubbing it into my palms and passing them over my hair and face.

The group began chanting *La ilaha illallah,* swaying their heads rhythmically from right shoulder to left. I followed along, as the repetition became faster, then shorter. *Illallah, illallah*—a sound that seemed like a human heart as heard from within the body. I began to feel slightly hypnotized, slightly euphoric, as the words were repeated perhaps one hundred times.

Zhati leaned over and explained *La ilaha illallah*—part of the universal declaration of faith repeated by all Muslims the world over—as I imagined a mystic might: "Other than God, there is nothing. Beyond all of the worldly deities our egos love to worship—ambition, power, wealth, social status, appearance—one Reality exists. Die to the old outmoded way of being that no longer serves the fullness of who we truly are."

Zhati adjusted the long string of prayer beads around her

neck and looked at me intently. "Die before you die. This is how we come to life."

After a while, the group rose and formed two concentric circles. Holding hands, we moved step over step to the left. A woman with a large frame drum and a man with a string instrument called a *setar* began playing, while another man entered the center of the circle and cupped a hand behind one ear. His voice rang out melodically in Arabic.

The group now seemed like a single beautiful organism, rippling along.

With Shaykha Fariha leading, everyone dropped hands and began to turn individually, slowly to the left, in the direction of the heart. Two women in flowing white skirts and a man with a long vest whirled faster and faster. I moved my feet out of their way, wondering if they ever got dizzy.

The dervishes spun for nearly fifteen minutes without pausing until, with a sudden clap of her hands, Shaykha Fariha brought their movement to an end. The whirlers crossed arms over chest and bowed their heads. They reminded me of figure skaters who manage to end a performance in a graceful steady pose after having spun so fast their pirouetting bodies seemed in danger of turning permanently rubberized.

The *zikr* ended after midnight. I was exhausted yet feeling completely alive. The smell of rose water, the light streaming from the chandeliers, the sounds of voices and music, and the meditative movement had captivated me, and I knew I would come back someday.

But what my experience that night would have to do with being called to the bedside of a dying Muslim man three months later, I would never have been able to say.

Mr. R was lying in a fetal position, facing the door. Even though he was covered with a sheet, I could tell that his frame was tall and skeletal. And he was shaking uncontrollably.

I dragged the heavy beige upholstered chair closer to the side of his bed and sat on its arm.

"Mr. R, my name is Barbara." No response. "If it's okay with you, I thought I would just sit here with you for a while."

His shaking was unnerving. I could almost feel my own brain rattling in my skull as I watched his body convulse. I leaned in closer to his bed and impulsively began humming, every bit as much to soothe myself as to soothe him.

When my own song was finished, I heard another verse from my memory. Faintly at first, *La ilaha illallah*—the Arabic incantation the Sufis had repeated over and over during their gathering—formed in my ears. They were the same words I had heard echo through the alleys of Dhaka while I was working in Bangladesh, and everywhere we had traveled in Turkey, as part of the prayer called from minarets five times each day.

I leaned closer to Mr. R and from the depths of my heart whispered the sacred words: *La ilaha illallah*. Nothing, only this.

After several rounds of repetition, I began to wonder about

him. What was the cause of his shaking? Where was his family? Did it matter, when no one else was available, that I wasn't Muslim? The beauty of the ancient phrase drowned my questions before I could formulate my guesses. None of the answers seemed worthy of this moment. *La ilaha illallah.*

Eventually I noticed that Mr. R's shaking had stopped. When I moved away from the bed, his body began to convulse wildly again, so I continued with the rhythm. *La ilaha illallah. La ilaha illallah.* I hadn't expected the chant to affect me as much as it did. He stopped being the unwell person and I the well one. The one in need of help and the helper. He a man, I a woman. He older, I younger. What could possibly be the use of divisions like that?

An hour and a half must have passed. I had to leave to go to work. His eyes were still closed, and he was still not responsive. But I told him how sorry I was to have to leave anyhow. As his shaking began again, I backed out of the room very slowly, not wanting to turn away from him for even a moment. It was wrenching to leave him this way.

When I switched on my computer at my desk an hour later, I was surprised to see an email from the volunteer whose shift followed mine:

I hope you are well! I wanted to tell you that when I came onto the floor, I saw the note you had written about a patient—that you stayed with him for a long time, humming. I wanted to let you know that when I saw that note I

*went to go see him, and it seemed he had passed just before
I got there. So you were there just before he died, you're the
last person he was with. I'm sure it was so helpful for him to
be with you and maybe you helped him to let go.*

*Anyway, I thought I'd let you know because sometimes
I find it's not so clear what's happened to a patient when
they're not there the next week, and it seemed like you had
a connection with him.*

I leaned back in my chair, overwhelmed with emotion. My
connection with Mr. R had been so short, but the length of our
meeting had hardly mattered. There seemed to be a place beyond
time, and we had met there with offerings to each other. His had
been a tremendous gift of illuminating our interconnectedness,
and all I wanted to do was to thank him for allowing me to join
him for a while. I opened the window by my desk, turned my
face into the cool breeze, and breathed his name.

TWO TURTLES

One March, Dave and I took a quick trip to Florida. We hadn't vacationed alone together in years. On our first day, we meandered along a secluded beach in an island state park on the Gulf of Mexico, holding hands like old times.

"Wouldn't it be something if we saw a sea turtle crawl out of the water?" I asked, feeling an odd sense of certainty that we would.

"Yup, that would be cool," Dave answered, adding reasonably, "Pretty unlikely, though."

As we approached the tip of the island, where the gentle swells of the gulf met the placid waters of the sound, I spotted a large dark figure at the water's edge. I could just make it out—the yellowish-brown shell and four flippers of a sea turtle. We came within fifteen feet of it and stopped, watching the hulking creature in silence.

"This is amazing," Dave whispered, as the turtle seemed to study us with knowing eyes. It had an air of nobility about it, like the wise old tortoise Master Oogway in our favorite family movie, *Kung Fu Panda*. Sometimes, to lighten the mood in our house, one of us would dramatically intone Oogway's sage lines,

Yesterday is history, tomorrow is a mystery, but today is a gift. That is why it is called the present.

"I think it's dying," I told Dave, thinking it strange that the turtle made no efforts to turn from us and swim back into the blue-green waters. We sat down in the sand, as if in vigil for this great being of the sea.

After twenty minutes or so, a ranger arrived. "This is very unusual," he said. "You don't see loggerheads on the beach during the day."

"It's dead," I said sadly, for now I noticed a change in its eyes.

"Yes, so it is," he said, tapping it with the toe of his boot. "Damn speedboats," he said, pointing to a large purple bruise on the turtle's thick neck, where it may have violently met the hull of a boat. "That and all the plastic they ingest."

I looked down at the turtle and thought again of Master Oogway. In one of the most beautiful cinematic depictions of an aware death, the elderly tortoise dissolves in a flurry of peach-tree blossoms that float up and join the energy of the cosmos. Dave, the boys, and I would cry right along with the movie from within the nest of blankets and pillows we created on the family room floor, mourning the loss of the animated tortoise.

We lose things all the time that aren't people. Jobs, precious objects, beloved pets. Death in the natural world weighs heavily too. A water source dried up. A forest lost to fire. An entire species gone extinct. Much of it is of our own doing. Increasingly, destruction isn't some remote happenstance, like something you read about in a far-off place but think would never happen to you. I learned that firsthand during Hurricane Sandy.

The evening before the superstorm made landfall in our area, I stood under the full moon at the East River on the Lower East Side. The high tide was already lapping over the edge of the esplanade. There was nowhere for the anticipated surge of stormwater to go but through the park, over the highway, and into our neighborhood. Dave was across the river in Brooklyn, making sure that everything was secured at his office. A few hours later, we would be separated from him as high winds closed the bridges and the country's largest transit system ground to a halt. Overnight, our region was thrown into the chaos of an unprecedented natural disaster.

Throughout the blackout of the following week, the boys and I would carry cases of water distributed by National Guard trucks up flights of stairs to the elderly and homebound in our neighborhood. I discovered there was a world of difference between the response to a man knocking on an apartment door in the pitch black saying, "I'm here to check on you" and when I tried it in my singsong voice. "Hi! I'm your neighbor! I have water for you," I'd call out gently, usually eliciting the sound of the chain and dead bolts being tentatively opened from the inside.

We were lucky, considering the loss of life and billions of dollars of property damage throughout our region. Over in New Jersey, my brother, who lives with his wife and children in the home where my grandparents once lived, came close to being crushed to death when a massive oak tree toppled and crashed onto their roof, clear through the support beam of the house and into the family room, precisely where he had been sitting with a distraught neighbor only seconds earlier. He and his family spent the night in a neighbor's dirt-floor basement, listening in terror as solid trees got caught in the path of a microburst and fell like dominoes all around them. The following morning, they salvaged what they could and moved in with my parents. The structural damage to the house took over a year to repair. Some nights, after a long day of manual labor, my brother would return to my parents' covered in sheep wool—the farm-grown insulation that my grandparents had used in their attic to keep the house warm.

What could we do in the face of large-scale destruction, Dave and I would often wonder together. We told the boys that our individual actions to care for the environment mattered—composting, recycling, hanging our clothes instead of putting them in the dryer. While hardly enough, these were actions that felt age-appropriate for the boys and some degree better than wringing our hands or turning a blind eye.

Years later, memories of Sandy and an urgent sense that catastrophic events would only increase over time propelled me to become certified as a disaster chaplain. I had many years of loss and life between those points in time, but it was the words of the ancient Jewish sage Rabbi Tarfon, whom Dave liked to quote, that got me started: *It is not your responsibility to finish the work of perfecting the world, but you are not free to desist from it either.*

On our last day in Florida during that short March break, I took a walk on a beach along the Atlantic Ocean, on the other side of the state from the gulf, a morning saunter to see the sunrise. An old man with long gray hair approached me from the opposite direction.

"Look over there," he said, as he pointed to the dunes behind him. "For some reason, I think you'll appreciate this."

There it was—another sea turtle. A leatherback this time, bigger than any turtle I'd ever seen. She had crawled out of the sea, leaving tracks as wide as an ATV on her journey to safe land. She was laying eggs the size of Ping-Pong balls. Well over a hundred eggs, the ranger who approached me later would say.

"Funny," he said. "Turtles usually lay their eggs at night, between ten and two, so the hot sun won't burn their backs. We'll get a mesh cage around the nest to protect the eggs from predators."

I nodded and thanked him.

Pay attention with new eyes, my inner voice urged. *The cycle of life and death is absolutely everywhere.*

With each experience, I continued to learn. That everything dies. That endangered species will disappear forever. That our neighborhood may very well be under water someday.

But the story of death can also be a story of the present

Last moments of the turtle
Caladesi Island State Park, Florida

moment. Be a *non-anxious presence* to whatever is before you, the seasoned disaster chaplains would say. In the face of the hardest things we will experience, be as a boulder in a rushing mountain stream. Listen. Take your time. The next move will emerge from the stillness. This is how we go forward, step by step, infusing darkness with light.

M aybe it should go without saying that there are not always tidy endings on the hospice floor. The more time I spent with the dying, the more I knew that my interactions with them would sometimes miss the mark, occasionally completely.

The day I was kicked out of the room by a hospice patient was one of the more memorable I had on the unit. Everyone who has done this work for any length of time will warn that some kind of radical rejection is inevitable, almost like a rite of passage. We prepare for the unpredictable, but somehow I was just hoping it would never happen to me.

Earlier in the day, I had heard a new patient, Mr. K, moaning and yelling from far down the hall, so I thought I would go in and try to talk to him. He was a huge man, perhaps six foot four. Multiple rounds of chemotherapy hadn't diminished his bulk. Lying flat on his back, he motioned for me to come closer.

As I stepped near his bedside, I noticed a large tumor on the side of his jaw. Whenever I encountered a patient whose illness was visible in some outward way, I held their gaze softly and smiled, just as I would for anyone else. I noticed that the skin of his brow was smooth and imagined his mother gently wiping his forehead when he was a child. I was prepared to love him.

Mr. K shifted his focus toward the landline telephone on his bedside table. "I want to talk to my wife, but I can't move a single muscle of this goddamned body," he roared.

I picked up the phone; there was no dial tone. I crawled under his bed and checked the connection. Still dead.

Determined to help, I told him I'd be back in a few minutes. I switched out a phone from an empty room, cleaned it with rubbing alcohol, and brought it to Mr. K. He watched me while I dialed the number written on a yellow pad on the bedside table.

A woman answered. "Mrs. K?" I asked. "Yes," she replied. I told her that I was a volunteer and that her husband wanted to speak with her. She said "very well" with such resignation that I could almost picture her tired eyes closing.

I put the phone to one ear of Mr. K's bald head, and he cried out her name like a small child. "How are you doing, S?" he asked, his voice quivering. I didn't catch her response, but she seemed to want the conversation to end quickly. After a minute, they said their goodbyes. Mr. K looked out the window and sighed. I was glad I had found a simple solution to his challenge.

The next moment, he abruptly shifted his focus and fixed his eyes on me. "There's a rubber band on my wrist, and it's cutting off my blood flow. I need you to cut it off right now," he demanded. I looked at his arm and saw the plastic hospital wristband with his name, birth date, and an ID number. Actually, it was two wristbands taped together to fit over his enormous forearm.

"That's the ID the nurses need to be sure they're giving you the proper medication, so I can't cut it off. . . ."

I was about to suggest I ask about having it switched to his other arm, but before I could, he bellowed, "You are *useless*! Useless and *pathetic*! Get the *hell* out of my room!" The blood vessels on his neck were popping out. It seemed plausible that if he had been able to move, his hands would have been around my throat in mere seconds.

I stood there amazed by the force of his anger. In contrast to the state of his body, it felt full of coursing life. My heart was pounding, and a flicker of shame glowed inside me.

I remembered my supervisor telling me about the first time she was kicked out of a patient's room. She had stood there like a deer in the headlights when the patient spat out, "What part of 'leave' are you too stupid to understand?" Patients couldn't easily tell off doctors or nurses, she told me, so you could see why asking volunteers to leave represented the only remaining control they had in their lives.

"I'm sorry, Mr. K," I said, shaken. "What a ridiculous thing—to not be able to help you with this. Let me get someone who can make it happen."

And so I left. I stepped across the carpet out of the room, willing myself not to take it personally. Imagine not being able to call a loved one, I reasoned. The embarrassment of having your intimate moment shared with a stranger. Your partner being unavailable for you when you needed them the most. Imagine being in a hospital—a place that is supposed to make you well—but no one can fix your creeping paralysis and pain. Imagine knowing that your remaining time could be measured in weeks, if not days.

My job was to be present and not to judge this man, whose identity was literally cutting off his circulation. And I knew that this wasn't about me or what I believed. It never was. As the theologian and writer Thomas Merton said, *Our job is to love others without stopping to inquire whether or not they are worthy.*

A nurse, hearing the commotion, came and asked if I was okay. "I am," I said. "But please check on his wristband when you can. It might need adjusting."

A week later I went back to visit Mr. K, hoping not to change things but to hold space for him to be however he needed to be—angry or sad, afraid or bitter. I wouldn't try to push him along to "acceptance" or "being at peace," I told myself. Instead, I would meet him where he was, exactly as he was, human to human. And if he wanted me to leave again, so be it. Only when I went in, the bed was freshly made and Mr. K was gone.

Sometimes I still visit Mr. K in my dreams. *Tell me where it hurts,* I ask him. Silently, he puts his enormous hand on his heart. *I'm sorry,* I tell him, my own heart aching along with his. *Is it easier now?* I ask him. I want so badly to hear what he has to say, but he always vanishes before he can answer. The story may never be complete.

GENEROUS BEAR

Do you think a place can hold pain?" I asked my friend over coffee at our neighborhood café, just two blocks from where a young man had been shot on the sidewalk the week before.

He put down his mug and studied my face. "Of course it can," he replied matter-of-factly. His long salt-and-pepper hair was pulled back in a ponytail and topped by a wide-brimmed hat with a colorful beaded band.

Known as Generous Bear, he is one of the people I trust the most when it comes to taking my musings seriously. Descended from the Muscogee Nation, whose people once spanned much of the southeastern United States, he is considered by many to be a wise elder. In a place like New York City, where reason and empirical evidence rule the day, Generous Bear can always be relied upon to see things differently.

"Places do hold memory. Any place in particular you're thinking about?"

"You know where the man was shot in broad daylight last week?" I asked. Generous Bear had heard the gunshots from his apartment. "The suspect was caught in the park right around the corner, in Corlears Hook. Something's not right with that place," I said.

"That's why I don't go there," he responded.

I first met Generous Bear at a workshop he was leading on indigenous spirituality. When we discovered we were neighbors, he warmly invited me to ceremonies he occasionally held in his apartment, one block from mine. His home feels more like a sacred lodge than a co-op on the Lower East Side. Feathers—symbols of protection and of seeing things from a wider perspective—adorn the four corners of his living room. Original ceremonial objects from Native groups that had adopted Christianity and, as a matter of acceptance and survival, distanced themselves from rituals of their past are meticulously cared for by Generous Bear in his home until someone comes forward to reclaim the tradition of their ancestors.

I could listen to him talk for hours about these objects and about his belief in the interdependent web of all existence that can be found by living in harmony with the natural world. The fact that we live in a city doesn't bother him in the least. He sees the earth element in the stones that make up our buildings, the water element in the ubiquitous water tanks above, the wind element in the gusty breezes rushing down the avenues, and the fire element in the electricity that lights our homes. To Generous Bear, everything involving Mother Earth is sacred.

"I did a little digging," I continued.

Digging came naturally to me. I was constantly struck by how similar I was to my father in the way I need to get my bearings, to understand the place where I live. To walk with my father was to learn about the geology and natural formations of the land, about which rocks were carved by glaciers, which rose from an ancient sea. The same is true of me and history. I could hardly stroll through my neighborhood without sensing who lived there before. I knew the precise location of Dave's grandfather's candy store, even though a modern apartment building now stands in its place. I knew that the synagogue across from our apartment was once a stopping point on the Underground Railroad. I imagined Manhattan, derived from the Lenape word meaning "the land of many hills," covered with wild blueberry bushes and fields of strawberries. Each morning, walking through Corlears Hook Park to the East River, I considered how the concrete promenade had once been shallow marshland, valued by the first inhabitants as an easy place to land a canoe.

During the course of my digging, I told Generous Bear, I had uncovered a little-known fact of neighborhood history: Corlears Hook was the site of a brutal massacre of the Native peoples who had set up an encampment there in 1643.

Generous Bear was nodding his head. He took a sip of coffee and put it down again, giving me his full attention. I told him the details I had learned.

On a single winter's night, Dutch soldiers carried out double attacks on Native encampments at both Corlears Hook and Pavonia, five miles away. More than 120 men, women, and children were slaughtered.

One Dutch settler's gruesome account remains. In the dead

of night, infants were torn from their mothers' breasts and hacked to pieces, their remains thrown into the fire or the river. Their parents, who tried to save them, were drowned. Those who survived had been maimed, hands and legs cut off. Some, who held their own entrails in their arms, came out from their hiding places and begged for help. They too were murdered.

After the bloodbath, things only got worse. Local indigenous groups carried out ferocious revenge attacks. Eventually, Corlears Hook was converted into shipping yards, attracting gangs and brothels. (One theory has it that the slang term *hooker* was used by sailors to refer to the prostitutes at Corlears Hook.) In 1832 the area housed a notorious makeshift cholera hospital, where ninety-three people died in a two-month period of time. Later the land became the site of New York's first tenement buildings for newly arrived immigrants. Today it is a park, bordered by affordable housing, which, at sea level, is vulnerable to flooding during storms like Hurricane Sandy. Altogether, the location had a chain of history that made the shooting of the week before seem almost expected.

"Not even a plaque marks this place," I concluded.

When I was finished talking, Generous Bear sat back in his chair and was silent. Finally, he spoke.

"Do places hold pain? Yes. In the same way that trauma in our bodies can reappear years later. That's also why we build memorials in Auschwitz, in Rwanda, in Cambodia. Why parallel towers of light are beamed into the night sky each year on

the anniversary of September 11. It's important to properly acknowledge the people who have suffered on these spots."

He looked up toward the ceiling and then back at me. "Well,
now that we know all of this history, we will do a small ceremony there."

I wasn't at all surprised by Generous Bear's suggestion of a
ceremony. The summer before, he had encouraged me to join a
delegation of Zen practitioners who flew to South Dakota to
meet with Lakota elders. "You must go," Generous Bear had
said. "The only passport you'll need is a sincere heart and an
open mind." I readily accepted the opportunity.

For a week, I traveled around the *Paha Sapa,* or Black Hills,
with the group's Lakota hosts. Each morning, we visited sites
that were considered holy or historically important to the community. Then we would gather in a circle under the shade of a
large cottonwood tree.

I had never before seen a cottonwood tree and was delighted
by how the white cottony tufts blew in the breeze, making it
look like it was snowing in July. When you cut a new branch off
the tree, one woman showed me, you would find a five-pointed
star. I could hardly believe it. Right there in the center of the
branch was a perfect little star. "It's the morning star," she said.
"A sacred source of healing."

The trip had been described as a "bearing witness" retreat.

This meant that our job as visitors was to listen with every fiber of our being to the stories our hosts shared, without judgment or expectation that anything in particular would happen as a result of our listening.

The elders told us about their way of life, their beliefs, and the reality of living on the reservation. Their generosity in sharing their stories, past and present, astounded me. When the *wasi'chu,* often used to refer to those of European descent, found gold in the Black Hills, they broke treaty agreements with the Northern Plains nations in order to take control of the land. They murdered legendary chiefs in cold blood and pushed their people onto desolate reservations. They took Native children away from their parents to reeducate them in far-off boarding schools. They polluted the land and waters when they found uranium and other resources and extracted them from the ground. Our hosts also told us about the impact of that history on the present and of the friends and family who had fallen to addiction and suicide.

I couldn't see how "bearing witness" was going to help any of this.

On our final day, we were invited to attend a private ceremony of the descendants of the Wounded Knee Massacre. On December 29, 1890, the U.S. Cavalry surrounded and attacked a Lakota encampment, killing more than 250 unarmed men, women, and children. Our gathering spot was the cemetery marking their mass grave atop a hill on the Pine Ridge Reservation.

I had expected a slick national monument, but as we walked through the humble brick gate topped by a small cross, I understood that it was up to the descendants to maintain the site. Prayer ties—strips of cloth in bright red, blue, yellow, and white—hung from the surrounding chain-link fencing, adding a quiet dignity to the windswept landscape.

The descendants offered prayers in Lakota and English. I caught the name of Lost Bird, an infant survivor whose story I had read. Four days following the massacre, she was discovered alive under her mother's frozen body and was adopted as a curio by a white soldier. "Adopted" felt like a nice word for "stolen," I thought as I learned of her lifelong struggles in a culture that held nothing but disdain for hers. It was only in more recent years that her remains had been returned to the Wounded Knee cemetery.

Someone handed me a pinch of dried tobacco, a sacred plant to First Peoples across the continent, to place on the grass covering the grave. I stood on the narrow concrete path and bent down with the offering, careful not to step on the hallowed ground.

A man approached on the walkway and ceremoniously handed me a plastic bottle containing the juice of the choke-cherry fruit to sprinkle on the grave as an offering to the ancestors. He looked right at me, then quickly lowered his eyes to the ground and said, "*Wóphila*. Thank you for coming." I tipped the bottle and watched as the bloodred liquid was absorbed by the dry earth, then passed it to the next person. When the commemoration ended, we paid our respects, filing past the descendants and their families, shaking every person's hand. I tried my hardest to remain collected, to not appear weak in the face of their steady composure.

Afterward, the descendants invited us to lunch in a church hall on the reservation. I sat down with a bowl of traditional stew and fry bread at a long table with three generations of one family. Two little girls tried to teach me to count from 1 to 10 in Lakota and doubled over in laughter as I mangled the pronunciation. I laughed too.

Something really does happen when we bear witness to the lives of others. It may not be apparent at first, but in time, something shifts. I could no longer see only distress and darkness, because pleasure and light were present as well. It was like watching sudden hailstorms in the Black Hills, followed by impossibly bright blue skies. Like being aware of the teen sleeping in an alley in Rapid City, as well as the young girl blessing the cottonwood tree to be used as the center pole in a traditional Sun Dance. Like noticing a mud-caked pickup truck spewing exhaust alongside a group of young people on horseback reviving the long-distance rides of their ancestors from centuries ago.

With all of this contradiction comes a far richer understanding—one not based on knee-jerk pity or some romanticized version of Native American life. It is from this more balanced place, the Zen and Lakota leaders were teaching me, that meaningful action can happen.

By evoking the past in this manner, we had collectively made way for a different kind of future. If that could happen on a hillside in South Dakota, where the great-great-grandson of the U.S. Cavalry commander at Wounded Knee would one day formally apologize to the Lakota descendants, maybe something worthy could also happen at a riverside park on the Lower East Side of Manhattan.

Walking beside Generous Bear to Corlears Hook, I was reminded of how intimately he knew suffering. He leaned heavily on his cane, his shoulders hunched slightly forward. His body had endured so much over the years, from late-stage kidney failure, which had nearly killed him until a donor kidney came through, to two brain surgeries. In two weeks, he would undergo surgery for prostate cancer. And just a few days earlier, his brother had been given less than six months to live. Generous Bear took all of it in stride, reminding me that the buffalo doesn't run from blizzards but lowers its boxy head and faces whatever comes its way, straight on.

He had invited along a woman named Terra, who lived part of the year with indigenous communities in Ecuador and Peru. She knew a thing or two about healing, Generous Bear said.

When we arrived at Corlears Hook, he took off his hat and surveyed the scene. It was late morning on a weekday, and the park was empty. "Every hair on my arms is standing straight up," Terra said, showing me her goosebumps in spite of the warmth of the day. On a park bench overlooking the river, Generous Bear took out the elements of ritual from his bag. Sage to purify and cleanse the area by smudging. A whistle made from bone. A stone blade.

He handed me several large leaves of dried tobacco. They were yellowish in color, and I inhaled their sweet earthy scent. "Break off pieces and lay them around the area, near the trees," he told me. "And just offer words from your heart."

I walked down a sloped hill toward a cluster of trees at the river's edge. I wanted to offer a profound prayer but found no words. Instead, I started humming a wordless song that arose from within.

I wound my way between the trees, remembering not only the victims of the massacre that had taken place on this land but also those who had died of cholera in the nearby hospital and those whose lives had been upended by violence in the past and today. In the distance, I could hear Generous Bear praying in Muskogee and occasionally piercing the air with the high-pitched bone whistle, calling out to the Great Spirit. Terra was playing a traditional honor song that Generous Bear had taught her on her wooden flute.

I thought of my friend Jen, who serves as a chaplain in a facility for formerly homeless adults, many with a history of mental illness and substance abuse. It's her job to conduct the memorial service when one of them dies. Even if no one shows up, she said, she will go ahead with it anyhow, speaking the blessings to the empty chairs. It's an act that changes her just as

Generous Bear, New York City
(Photograph by Jennifer Silacci)

much as it honors them, she told me. This is what our ceremony by the river felt like for me too.

Three young men in suits walked by on their way south toward the Financial District. I could only guess what they thought of our ritual. As for myself, it didn't matter to me how our ceremony worked or even *if* it worked in any quantifiable way. All I knew was that the act of bearing witness here, on my home turf, felt like an important first step.

As I made my way back up the hill to rejoin Generous Bear and Terra, I felt the sun on my face and looked up toward the clear spring sky. One of the red-tailed hawks nesting in the area was circling high above, offering its wider vision.

DAD

A round the time of Dave's and my wedding, my father was diagnosed with prostate cancer. It had been detected early and handled quickly. By all medical estimations, he would die of something else long before prostate cancer would ever reappear and become an issue again.

Now, well into his eighties, he had a routine test of his PSA levels, and his urologist discovered that his numbers had shot back up. Along with that, he was experiencing severe pain in his back. My mother called, sounding uncharacteristically rattled.

"I don't want to talk too loudly, or I'll wake up your father," she whispered into the phone. "He's not doing well. He cries out in pain all night long. Next week his doctor wants to do a bone scan to see if the cancer spread."

I offered to take my father to his appointment.

At six-thirty in the morning, at the hospital where my father had worked for most of his career, I filled out the paperwork for tests that would take a good portion of the day. A young technician injected a small amount of radioactive tracers into my father's left arm and told us we would need to wait while the solution traveled to his spine, allowing them to capture a reliable image of what was going on. We should be back for the bone scan in three hours.

Eyeing the crowded waiting room with a hint of displeasure, Dad said, "Follow me," and took off with his cane toward the elevator.

People with Alzheimer's disease often remember precise details from their store of long-term memory, and the halls of this hospital were no exception for my father. He led me to the lobby, then down a glass corridor to an older wing of the building.

He paused in front of an official-looking door with a keypad of numbers above the knob. I wondered what was inside and if Dad could possibly remember the code, assuming it hadn't been changed in the intervening years. A minute passed, and a doctor in a white coat opened the door from the other side. My father caught it as the doctor exited, then smiled widely at me and said, "Come on in," like he owned the place.

The entry opened into a private lounge area for the hospital's medical staff. A kitchen in the corner was stocked with coffee, tea, pastries, and bagels. Comfortable couches and armchairs were arranged around a table loaded with current magazines. Staff mailboxes lined the walls near a couple of computer work-stations, where a few doctors in blue operating room scrubs checked their email.

Dad headed for the coffee.

"I don't think we should be in here," I whispered nervously, looking around the room.

"Like hell we shouldn't be," he said, gingerly picking out a cherry Danish with plastic tongs. "What can I get you?"

I rolled my eyes like I was a teenager again and took his hot drink over to the couch. Looking pleased, he settled in with his snack, picked up a *National Geographic,* and stared at the pictures. Not wanting to create a scene, I took out my laptop and plugged it into the outlet behind Dad's chair. I could see the staff over by the computers looking our way. Their looks felt laced with judgment, and I was embarrassed.

"Dad, does this room look exactly like when you worked here?" I asked loudly, hoping they would overhear me and understand that we belonged.

"Uh-huh," he mumbled over his steaming cup.

I opened a blank email and began writing to my friend Wendy, who is in charge of the counseling department at a college.

I explained to her where we were and that I thought we should leave. I clicked send and waited for her response, looking up at the clock on the wall by the door. Two and a half hours to go.

Wendy's message arrived shortly after I reached out to her. *Stay right where you are,* she wrote. *Your dad knows exactly where he belongs. Maybe it will teach the younger docs a thing or two about how life happens to everyone—that vigor is necessary for the intensity of medicine, but humanity must accompany that, always.*

I looked over my laptop screen. Dad was falling asleep. I took his half-full coffee cup from his hands and put it on the table. I took a shallow breath.

Wendy? I wrote again. *I've been feeling kind of breathless lately. I think it may be anxiety.*

Everything that was happening felt upside down. My dad had become like a child, and I like his parent. I was losing him before I lost him.

Anxiety would make perfect sense, she wrote back. *It can feel awful, really, and does not respond to "blocking it out" or distraction. To the contrary, often leaning into each and every physical, emotional, and psychological experience you are having can help tremendously.*

After a pause of several minutes, during which I could envision her calming a stressed-out college student, she continued: *Try to think about each symptom as attempting to communicate an important message: If you are having trouble taking a deep breath, consider how the body is trying to remind you that you must breathe more intentionally throughout all of this. If your legs tense up, think about all the ways they are preparing you to run, and explore what it is that you are running from—sadness, fear, resentment. It's an exquisitely sensitive system designed like an alarm. If you are not registering some aspect of danger it will get louder and louder until it's convinced you are. Welcome it all.*

I took a deeper breath and rolled my neck a few times in each direction. The great surgeon was now sound asleep, and the young doctors had turned their attention back to their computer monitors.

You have some of life's hardest situations around you right now, Barbara—transition, illness, anticipated loss. That's like swimming in a sea of what folks dread most in life. Gosh, I hate that you are surrounded by this all. Fill your days with honest conversations and plenty of rest. And, knowing you as I do, a piece of chocolate too.

I laughed a little at her last sentence. Knowing that I had a friend who understood me on so many levels put my mind at ease a bit. It occurred to me that one doesn't learn much resilience when life goes "right" most of the time. It was this moment—the one that was testing me to the core—where the potential for growth lay.

When the three hours had passed, Dad and I went back upstairs to the still-crowded waiting room and sat in the hard leatherette seats. After a few minutes, the technician called Dad's name. He helped my father walk across the room and suggested I remain in the waiting room. I absently watched the television broadcast of continuous news clips.

After about thirty minutes, my father reemerged. He seemed distant, as if he had fallen asleep during the procedure.

"Your doctor will call you next week with the results," the technician said, patting Dad on the back. I scanned the technician's face, looking for a hint as to what he found, but could tell nothing.

Back in the car, I buckled my father into the passenger seat and then drove out of the parking lot and through the neighborhoods adjoining my childhood home. I remembered him telling me as a kid what it was like to head home after finishing a long surgery. "I'd smell fresh-cut grass and barbecues and hear children playing, and it would make me so happy to be coming home to our family."

"You know," Dad said finally, breaking the reverie, "I can't read words anymore. I know that. But I still know how to read a scan of the spine."

"So you were watching when he did the procedure?"

He nodded and looked out the window. "The news is not good. There are spots up and down my spine. But don't tell the lady of the house, please. It would really upset her."

I bit my lip to keep it from trembling. I wanted the roles to be reversed again, to pull the car over and be wrapped in his arms, seeking reassurance. Finally, I glanced over at him. "Okay, Dad," I said. "It will be between us for now."

I knew my mom would learn the news of the metastases in a few days, but somehow keeping his secret felt like the surest way to honor him. And I didn't know how many more opportunities I'd have like that.

Eight months later, it was my mother who was in the hospital for a pacemaker. It was a procedure that is, in most cases, relatively straightforward. But the one-hour surgery had turned into five hours, and in the process, her lung partially collapsed. It would take a few more days for her to recover.

I returned to my childhood home to stay with my father. To cook, to put in his eye drops three times a day. To bathe him, and to help him to bed. I even brought along the copy of *Walden* he had given me years before, thinking he'd like to hear it as he went to sleep. He wasn't interested. So I read him the children's book *Robin Hood* that my mother kept in a bookcase for her grandchildren, slowly turning the pages and showing him the pictures. He seemed particularly amused by the Disney version of the bumbling Sheriff of Nottingham.

One morning before breakfast, the short window of time each day when his mind was at its clearest, he turned to me from his seat on the couch and asked, "When's my birthday?"

His frame looked small under his red-and-white crocheted blanket, but his eyes were alert and fixed intently on mine.

"You'll be eighty-eight this summer," I told him.

He raised his eyebrows, as if surprised by the number, then paused to formulate his next words. "I'll try to make it till then, and then I'll slip away."

My breath froze mid-inhalation. I thought I should hug my father but stopped myself, knowing it would cut short the conversation about dying he seemed open to having right then and there. I sat down next to him and fought to compose myself.

"Dad, you've lived such a long and meaningful life, and you've touched so many people. You can feel great about that," I began. "You'll know when the time is right to let go."

"But do *you* think it's right?" he asked.

I noticed my lower lip quivering once again and bit it gently. How does a daughter who loves her dad answer a question like this? I knew that he was asking for nothing but my honesty.

"Yes, Dad," I replied finally. "I think the time is about right."

Those may have been the hardest words I ever uttered. I was

Dad, age eighty-seven, in his first selfie

surprised that I had held it together and felt a quiet relief in having spoken the truth.

Later that day, as I was unloading groceries from the trunk of the car, I noticed that I had bought my father V8 Original instead of Low Sodium. Only then did I lose it. I leaned against my car and sobbed uncontrollably over buying the wrong stupid V8.

Maybe we're not all destined to care for our parents' ailing bodies. Maybe we won't ever be called upon to answer their hardest questions. But I think we could all use V8 moments sometimes—moments when the small things become stand-ins for the larger ones, allowing the pain to begin its slow and inexorable release.

MRS. D, ROOM #710

Helen, Dave's father's cousin, was the life of any party, including my wedding. Standing at four and a half feet tall, she wore heels and a flapper dress with a long string of pearls and danced for hours while the rest of us looked on in amazement. She attributed her smooth complexion to a homemade concoction of strawberry seeds and cold cream. You would be forgiven for thinking she was half the eighty years she was.

As a kid, Dave spent a week every summer with his widowed grandfather Irving at Kutsher's, the legendary Catskills resort popular with Jewish Americans. Helen and her husband often joined them. She had a notable, sometimes dark sense of humor. One day, she joked with the younger family members that they should all start a greeting-card empire and challenged them to come up with unique verses. Everyone's favorite was her impromptu sympathy card:

Sorry to hear your husband is dead,
Thank goodness you found him lying in your bed.

A few kids reportedly sat on the sidewalk and wet their pants from laughing so hard.

The condolence card notwithstanding, everything about Helen spoke of life itself. While we only saw her every few years, we always looked forward to hearing about the next installment of her life.

Until one day I found her somewhere I didn't expect to find her.

I had walked into the single room across from the nurse's station belonging to a "Mrs. D," completely unaware. The woman in the bed was by herself but doing something I had only heard about during our hospice training—reaching out her hands and speaking with people she alone could see. It was more common than you would think, we had learned. In one study, over 80 percent of patients at the end of life experienced atypical visions or dreams, frequently involving long-lost loved ones. The woman didn't seem distressed by this interaction, as unintelligible as it was to me. Rather, it was as if she were having a delightful conversation with friendly beings on an entirely different plane.

I took a seat by Mrs. D's bedside. A soft lamp on the side table cast a warm glow onto her face. Her eyes were wide open, as if she were gazing into a place far more real than this one. I leaned in a little closer to study her unlined complexion. With a start, I saw that it was Helen.

I sat back, my heart pounding, as she continued her otherworldly speaking. No one in Dave's immediate family knew that Helen's health had taken a turn for the worse.

How old was Helen now? I did some quick math and realized she must be about ninety-seven. I reflected on this for a moment. The fact that I knew her made her mumbling feel more eerie than it had just moments before. Perhaps to distract myself, I thought of a practical consideration—there might be some hospital privacy rule about my being in a relative's room with access to her medical status without the knowledge of her next of kin.

I had stood to leave so I could discuss it with my supervisor when, in the stream of her speaking, Helen called out, "Irving."

Irving, Dave's grandfather Irving? Who else could it be? I wondered if this hospice work was beginning to get to my head. Yet I had heard the name as clearly as if it had been my own. Irving.

I moved toward the door, giving a wide birth to the unseen visitor—the long-departed man with a white mustache and enormous glasses whose photograph hung in our apartment. I had shivers when I remembered that not only was Irving's picture on our wall but that our apartment itself had been the very same home where Irving had once lived after he moved from a tenement on Delancey Street, eventually leaving it in his will to Dave. Our children were the fourth generation to live there.

By the following morning, the hospice unit had cleared it with Helen's son that I and any other family members could visit anytime. Her son apologized profusely—between his daily visits to the hospice floor and cleaning out the apartment Helen had just vacated, he simply hadn't had enough time to let us know that she had fallen ill. I was grateful for the positive family dynamic we had. A few times I had witnessed drawn-out familial arguments on the hospice floor. Once, a daughter and son fought about their inheritance over their sleeping father's body. I stood there in horror, watching what appeared to be age-old hurt feelings about who had been the favored child and who had felt unseen, until I had the wherewithal to offer them a small conference room down the hall to talk.

In the afternoon I returned to see Helen again, this time with Drew, whose school was closed for the Thanksgiving break. Drew wasn't thrilled about coming along, especially because Evan already had plans with friends. I promised that it would be a quick stop after getting his hair cut, not far from the hospital. If he didn't feel comfortable seeing her, I reassured him, he could sit in the hospice "family room"—the tastefully decorated living room for visitors with comfortable couches and an area with books and puzzles for kids.

"That sounds okay," he said, brightening when I told him about the unlimited supply of graham crackers and milk.

I had introduced the idea of hospice to the boys when I was learning the ropes. Dave and I told them the essentials—that hospice patients likely have less than six months to live and are receiving care to make them comfortable. I told them about how my grandmother had died at peace in my childhood home under the care of the nicest hospice workers you could ever meet.

That seemed to satisfy the boys. Their main misgiving about my work had been that the public hospital where I had been assigned was in the headlines as containing the first official New York City isolation unit for treating patients with the life-threatening Ebola virus. "That unit is completely sealed," I reassured them, telling them about the well-trained doctors and nurses in head-to-toe hazmat suits and the police stationed outside the floor. "There's no way I could just wander in. It's probably safer inside that hospital than any other place in the city," I said, hoping it was true.

After settling Drew into the family room, I walked down the carpeted hall to Helen's room. Again, I sat in the chair at her bedside, this time watching her sleep quietly. She wore pearl earrings, and her wavy white hair was neatly combed. I held her hand and hummed a little. After about fifteen minutes, I kissed her forehead and went to retrieve Drew.

I found him with two elderly women in cardigan sweaters, who were admiring his neatly groomed curly blond hair. They looked like they could be twins.

"I hope you don't mind," said the woman in the pink cardigan, "but we'd ordered in some pizza and we gave your handsome young man a slice."

"And a ginger ale too," the woman in the teal cardigan added. Drew was enjoying the attention. I laughed, thinking about the hospice's "Good Dog" program, in which volunteers bring trained therapy dogs to the bedside to soothe patients. Instead of a well-behaved pet, Drew was like the "Good Child" equivalent.

Drew waved goodbye to his new friends. On the way out of the family room, he said, "I might want to see Helen, if she doesn't have any tubes sticking out of her or anything. Because that would be gross."

After I explained that there was only a small, clear nose tube delivering oxygen to her lungs, we walked into the room.

"Helen, Dave's boy Drew is here," I announced. Helen's eyes remained closed. Drew stepped toward the bed.

"She's very cute," he whispered. She really was. "You kind of look like her," I told him, rustling his hair. He scowled and used his fingers to comb it back into place.

I wondered if the unseen people Helen had been talking to on my first visit were hanging around. A few months earlier I had met a patient from New Zealand who was part Maori. "The only thing bringing me peace," she had told me as she lay paralyzed from the chest down, "is knowing that the ancestors will be here at the end to help me transition. They'll be right here around my bed." Her words were never far from my mind when visiting patients. If there was even a remote possibility that Dave's ancestors were nearby for Helen, I couldn't waste this opportunity.

"Irving," I mouthed quietly so that Drew couldn't hear me—I could barely hear myself. "If you're here, I want you to meet your great-grandson Drew. Let's all look out for one another, okay?"

I half-expected an eerie breeze to rustle the curtains, but all was still. And that was just as well with me.

We carry our ancestors forward. They are in us and of us.

With the convergence of our lives—past and present—death is no longer a stark boundary. I can see this, feel this, as if it's some essential but oft-forgotten truth.

As we left the hospice floor, my arm around Drew's shoulder, I was grateful that I had brought him along. We headed in the direction of home, Irving's home too.

Helen died a few days later, right after Thanksgiving.

WATER CHILDREN

Hanging above the altar at Koshin and Chodo's Zen center are dozens of tiny, colorful paper cranes. Positioned above black-and-white photos of the departed masters of the Zendo's lineage, the cranes might seem slightly out of place, as if they are actually in flight.

But for Dave and me it makes perfect sense, for we had folded two of the origami birds into being as an act of remembrance for the daughters we had lost years before but had never fully acknowledged.

It was Chodo's idea to come together to honor the losses of children, born and unborn, in the community. In Japan, there is a ritual known as *mizuko kuyō* to honor the "water children." A water child, Chodo explained, represents the idea that life flows into being like liquid, from the moment of conception, into the waters of the womb, and through the flexibility of early childhood, until we become firmer and more durable. The loss of a water child is honored at any stage along the way, no matter through miscarriage, abortion, stillbirth, or the death of a young child. Through ritual, the Japanese bid them farewell, opening up to the possibility that in another time and place they may again come into existence.

The tradition was connected to a practice I had witnessed while living in Japan after college. In gardens surrounding Buddhist temples, I would often spot row upon row of little stone statues of the bodhisattva Jizo—an enlightened being who looks like a smiling baby himself. Jizo, sometimes dressed in a tiny red knitted cap and shawl, is the guardian protector of the water children. Families come to the temple grounds on a few occasions throughout the year to acknowledge their loss with their own personal Jizo. It can be a joyous time as they change the weather-beaten clothing and offer brightly colored pinwheels, candy, and folded notes before the statue. It struck me a little like the Mexican Day of the Dead, in which images and objects significant to the deceased are displayed for all to remember and celebrate a life that has passed. In Japan in my early twenties, still far from thinking of having a family myself, I thought the Jizo practice was sweet, in a Hello Kitty kind of a way.

There is, in our culture, a way in which the things that most need to be said are often the least likely to find expression. The death of an adult is difficult enough, but the loss of a child—a "what *could have* been"—is taboo. By not appreciating Dave's need to talk more openly about the loss of our daughters, I had asked silence of him as well.

The *mizuko kuyō* was not only about our unborn children but about the promise of healing the invisibility. Though our losses had happened more than a decade earlier, as soon as I saw the invitation to join the ritual, I knew it was what Dave and I still needed. It was my way to make up for the silence.

Twelve of us sat around the Zendo's cherry table—some who had experienced recent losses, others whose losses happened even longer ago than ours. Unless they wanted to, no one had to speak the name of their loss or somehow seek to justify it by defining at what stage it had happened. Instead, we would simply fold square paper. I could see Chodo's past life as an art director at play in the activity.

"Write a message inside if you'd like," he suggested to the group. Wordlessly, I took Arden, and Dave took Adele. In spite of all of the years that had passed, in my mind, Arden and Adele were growing up with Evan and Drew. If Evan was seventeen, Arden was eighteen. If Drew was fourteen, Adele was fifteen. Not finding words to express how alive they still felt to me, I drew a full heart instead on the blank side of the sheet. I leaned over to look at Dave's. *I wish I had the chance to know you,* he had simply written. He saw me looking and smiled tenderly. I reached for a tissue, feeling sorry again that I had asked him to tamp down his emotions so I wouldn't have to face mine.

There are twenty-two precise steps involved in making a paper crane, folding and unfolding, joining and separating, turning sideways, flipping upside down. As we worked, we'd catch a sniffle and the box of tissues would be passed silently down the row. We worked on our own, yet in community. It was a community that extended beyond this table, I knew. In talking to my mother about my miscarriage, I learned for the first time that she too had lost a pregnancy, a brother or sister who would have been the youngest in our family. My mother's mother had lost a two-day-old child. My father's mother had two or three miscarriages—no one could remember exactly. My maternal great-grandmother had died in childbirth along with her baby in a coal-mining town in Pennsylvania. I felt connected to a family story I hadn't known existed. And if this was the history of my family alone over just four generations, including me, how many countless millions shared in the world's unwritten epic of hidden sorrow?

It was nearly impossible to believe that the creasing and un-creasing would result in anything but a crinkly piece of fancy paper, but in the final step, I folded two flaps to a 90-degree angle and saw that I had created wings of a bird.

Finishing early, I hastily made another crane to bring home with us. It was lopsided and imperfect, but that felt honest. In-side was my message:

Arden and Adele: When you left, you pointed out a way for me to wake up. I'm still trying.

Thank you,
Mom

When everyone was finished, we followed Chodo into the meditation hall. One by one, we went forward to put our cranes before the altar. I watched as Dave carried his in both palms as if he were comforting a tiny bird dropped from a nest. In that moment, I loved him more than I thought it was possible to love another human being.

Jizo

To mark the closing of the ritual, Chodo recited the evening *gatha,* or meditative verse, which is chanted in a haunting monotone every night in Zen temples across the globe. I had heard it countless times, but this time, I could finally feel its promise.

> *Let me respectfully remind you*
> *Life and death are of supreme importance.*
> *Time swiftly passes by and opportunity is lost.*
> *On this night the days of our life are decreased by one.*
> *Each of us must strive to awaken.*
> *Awaken.*
> *Take heed.*
> *Do not squander your life.*

I reached over to take Dave's hand as we listened to the closing strikes of the temple bell.

TRACY, ROOM #700

On a cold gray morning, a series of events unfolded on the hospice floor that felt like more than just a coincidence.

I arrived early, before the floor manager, who was responsible for printing the ever-changing list of who had died the night before and who was newly arriving. Without this information, I went into rooms without knowing a patient's name, age, or diagnosis. I preferred it that way, to approach each threshold without any preconceptions. Then it was just them and me. A fresh moment. A clean slate.

That morning, I started at the first door at the end of the hall. A delicate Asian woman who looked to be in her late fifties lay seemingly unresponsive, her eyes closed, thick salt-and-pepper hair fanned out on her pillow. I stood at the side of her bed, took a chance, and introduced myself. I told her I would sit with her for a while and asked if she would like me to hold her hand. Slowly, a very thin yet elegant hand moved up from under her rose-colored blanket. I put my hand under hers, as I was trained to do, so that she could move her hand away if she wanted. So she'd remain in control.

I wondered who she was and what had brought her here.

I found myself singing "Edelweiss" to her softly, the song my mother loved to sing to my brothers and me when we were babies and that I, in turn, sang to my boys the first time I held them in my arms. *Edelweiss, edelweiss, every morning you greet me.*

The floor nurse came in to check her vitals. I told the woman in the bed that I would come back again before I left for the day. I visited every room on the floor that morning. When I finally had time to pick up a copy of the census at the front desk, I quickly scanned the list.

There was a column for PaySource, which listed the entity responsible for the bill: private insurance companies, Medicare, or Medicaid. One patient's insurance carrier jumped out at me, an unusual company with a Japanese name that I knew only because it was the same insurance as mine, which was offered through Dave's work. I looked across the row to the patient's name. It was the woman with the beautiful hands in the first room, a woman I could see now was named Tracy.

In an instant, I understood that this woman was a manager at Dave's company—a woman who had been a dedicated employee up until cancer prevented her from working any longer. Dave had visited her in the hospital and at home as the disease progressed. The boys and I had met her too, when they were little and we brought a big box of chocolates to the company's annual holiday party. I remembered that she had told Dave she wanted to find some good books on mindfulness, and I had passed along a few of my favorite titles.

I walked back into her room, feeling a sense of calm that outweighed the strange circumstance. Here we were, alone on a drab rainy morning, too early for her family to be there. Her breathing was shallow. I sat down and again placed my hand under hers. "Tracy, it's Barbara. It took me a little while to understand who you are. I'm Dave's wife, and I'm glad I could be here with you right now. Dave has spoken so highly of you over the years. How you've been such an important part of the team that you're like family."

I knew that to be true. I also knew that her own family was a loving one. Not every patient has a blanket from home, and I told her so.

I sat watching her silently, noticing the slow rise and fall of her breath. She had looked peaceful when I came in, but now I noticed her face relax completely. Her skin seemed to be draped smoothly over her high cheekbones.

"I am going to stay with you. No matter what is happening, I'm not afraid to walk with you." I hadn't planned to say this, but I meant it with every fiber of my being. I would stay here all day and all night if need be. All of the thinking and sorrows and joys of my life had led me to this moment, and I knew I belonged in this precise place, at this precise time.

Mary, the volunteer in charge of delivering fresh flowers, came in with a vase of chrysanthemums and placed it on the bedside table. A staff chaplain, Father Tom, poked his head in to see if we were okay. I nodded and told him we were.

Alone again, I noticed that I was syncing my breath to hers.

I started singing "Edelweiss" again, softly. *Blossom of snow may you bloom and grow, bloom and grow forever . . .*

About ten minutes passed. Tracy let out a forceful breath, like the air rushing out of a balloon. It was followed by a gentle breath in and then out. I waited for the next breath, holding my own, but that was all there was to be. In the most extraordinary of ordinary moments, Tracy passed away at 11:36 A.M.

I felt a great sense of peace wash over my body. Koshin and Chodo had often reminded us that death on a hospice ward isn't an emergency. There isn't a reason to frantically ring call buttons for help. So I sat with her for several minutes, my hand still touching hers, and thanked her for letting me be with her. In a city of millions of people with more than sixty hospitals, on my one morning per week on this unit, the first person I had been with at their last breath was someone I knew, however briefly.

I only noticed I was crying when I tasted the salty tears in my mouth. I smoothed her hair; her head still felt warm. I stood slowly and put my hands together in front of my heart. Then I went to inform the nurse.

At home that evening, Dave told me that Tracy's niece called him at work to let him know that Tracy had died. He had hesitated for a moment, then told her I had been volunteering on the floor that morning. The niece was silent at first and then asked if I would call her later. Dave was deeply saddened by Tracy's death, sorry that he hadn't had the chance to say a final farewell. He was also relieved that her pain was over. "I'm sorry, Dave," I said, putting my head on his shoulder.

The boys were listening carefully and wanted to know what happened to Tracy, whom they both remembered. I was wary of half-told, glossed-over, hushed-tone explanations of death—especially those that were secretive when children were present. I sat with them on the couch and with care recounted the morning. I searched their eyes and wondered how they would react.

"You sang 'Edelweiss' to her?" Evan asked, incredulous. I nodded.

"'Edelweiss'!" Drew echoed. "Mom! You probably killed her with that stupid song."

When I called Tracy's niece, I could hear her voice trembling. "My family wants to thank you for being there," she said after I explained what had happened. "We are wondering if she ever opened her eyes or said anything?"

"She looked peaceful, almost like she was sleeping," I said. "If there is such a thing as a beautiful death, she had it." Before we hung up, she invited Dave and me to the memorial service the following week.

The service was held in a funeral home tucked away on a small street in Chinatown. A man in a dark suit greeted us at the door, handing us each a piece of hard candy. "Eat it for sweetness on this day of sorrow," he said.

Inside, Dave and I stood side by side as another attendant in a suit handed us each a burning stick of incense. He instructed

us to bow three times at an altar, upon which was a large bowl
full of upright sticks of burning incense, a candle, three bowls
of water, a roast chicken in a tin pan, and offerings of oranges,
rice, and vegetables. I heard a recording of chanting in Chinese
being piped into the room. Then we were led behind the altar,
where Tracy was laid out in an open casket. She looked regal in
a traditional gold jacket, her hair in an elegant chignon. Her
eyeglasses, which I had noticed on her bedside table on the hospice unit, were now resting on the ledge inside the coffin. As
instructed, Dave and I bowed in unison three more times and
turned to greet the family one by one. "I'm so sorry," I said, looking into the eyes of each of them.

"Thank you for being with her at the end," her sister said.
"We can't tell you how much it means to us."

"It was an honor," I replied truthfully. If I told them that being with Tracy had felt like treading on sacred ground, I might
have cried all over again.

Her brother explained the elements of a traditional Chinese
funeral. He pointed to the front of the room, piled high with
objects that looked like children's toys. "They are meant as offerings for her afterlife," he said. I looked more carefully: a paper
model of a mansion the size of a large dollhouse, with many tiny
air-conditioning units and figurines of a maid and a butler out
front; a two-foot-long gold car; a pair of running shoes and a
pair of Chanel dress shoes; a faux Apple laptop; a replica of a
high-tech media system; a six-pack of soda; and wads of fake

green money. All of the objects were going to be burned in a small oven in the wall at the foot of the casket, the smoke reaching the spirit world in an act of supplication.

A friend of the family brought us a stack of square silver joss paper. She taught us to fold the paper into the shape of origami bars called "ghost money," which would also be burned as a form of prayer for a comfortable afterlife. I folded as quickly and carefully as I could, getting drawn into the idea that through this ritual the family's loss could be transformed into hope, their hardship into ease. Dave furrowed his brow in concentration and set to work as well.

When the wake ended, we were each handed a red envelope with a quarter inside and instructed to spend the money on the way home for good luck to offset the bad fortune of attending a funeral. Dave and I parted ways to go to work, and I began my walk to work through Chinatown. I opened the wrapper and popped the hard candy we'd been given into my mouth. I spent the quarter while buying a coffee at a local café full of young mothers with fancy strollers and twenty-somethings hunched over laptops. The barista smiled at me and for no reason put a free doughnut in my hand. I thought I'd save it for the boys, but all that was left were crumbs when I reached my destination.

A week later, I made an appointment to talk to Chodo. While I had felt serene in the moments before and after Tracy died, now it was different. Every time I tried to follow my breath in meditation, I couldn't get the vivid image of her final breath out of my head. It felt unsettling, as if I were breathing for her, or she for me.

I walked into the small interview room at the Zendo, which contained only a lamp and two chairs facing each other. "Have a seat," Chodo said in his deep voice, pointing to the most comfortable chair. I obeyed.

"Tell me what's been going on," he asked gently.

I blurted out the whole story, hardly pausing for breath. When I was done, I looked at his face and waited, feeling suddenly exhausted.

Chodo took off his glasses and stared at me. Finally he said, "That is mind-blowing!" He pointed at me for emphasis and continued, "Imagine the past karmas—yours and Tracy's—that brought you two together right as she was dying." I felt a great sense of relief that this monk—a man who had seen so much in his years of tending to the dying—seemed to see a greater meaning in what had happened. I could not hold back the tears anymore, nor did I want to.

"She was your teacher," he said softly, handing me a tissue. "She showed you that all we ever truly have is this one breath. Right here, right now. If all the training you've done was for this one moment with her, it all would have been worth it."

Chodo was right. Tracy was my teacher. What happened between us reminded me of Indra's net—an ancient Eastern symbol representing a vast, delicate web expanding infinitely in all directions. At each crossing point, there is a multifaceted jewel, and in each one, it's possible to see the reflection of all the others, mirroring one another without end. Tracy and I were like a single intersection of the net, and the instant our connection caught a glimmer of light, it was reflected out into the universe. Nothing fixed, nothing solid, nothing bound by time or place, nothing uniquely mine or hers. There was a tremendous sense of freedom in catching even a tiny glimpse of this web of interconnection, as if nothing existed outside its beautiful cosmic structure.

From the depths of that mysterious place, I could also pause and ground myself with a breath. The first act of a newborn is to breathe in; the last act of the dying is to breathe out—our entire life span, and that of anyone ever born or to be born, in a single cycle of a breath. What could be more worthy of attention?

MY PARENTS

On an afternoon in early September, Evan and I planned a Walden Pond do-over. It had been many years since our first visit, when we were forced to turn back after his little body doubled over and he retched on the path that wound its way to the site of Thoreau's cabin. That unfortunate incident had become the stuff of family lore, and this time we were out to create a new narrative.

We had been touring prospective colleges in Boston all day and managed to arrive at the water's edge as the sun was beginning its descent into the tree line. The sky over Walden Pond was magnificent in its vibrant pink, orange, and blue. It occurred to me for the first time that, as much as my father loved *Walden,* he had never been to the pond himself. Knowing that his life was ebbing made me doubly determined to make this visit count.

Evan was in an upbeat mood; the next step of his life journey was about to begin. I felt a giddy sense of anticipation for him as we took off our shoes, rolled up our pants, and waded out into the waters. A line from *Walden* came to mind: *If one advances confidently in the direction of his dreams, and endeavors to live the life which he has imagined, he will meet with a success unexpected in common hours.*

The following morning began as expected. Evan was in his first college interview and was scheduled to sit in on a class afterward and then meet the professor. It was a useful opportunity for him to learn more about the school and demonstrate his interest. But as I was passing the time waiting for him in the college bookstore, a strong feeling overwhelmed me. It had no voice, but if it had, it would have said, *Leave here now. Go to your father.*

I picked up Evan outside the admissions office. "Get in the car," I said, handing him the sandwich I had bought at the campus cafeteria.

"But what about the class?" he wanted to know.

"I'm sorry," I said. "It's just a hunch that something is going to happen soon."

We drove the interstates from Massachusetts to New Jersey, over four hours away, pushing the speed limit the entire way. I realized that dropping everything to follow a strong instinct must have seemed reckless to Evan. The end was certainly nearing for my father, but, for all any of us knew, he could be with us days or weeks more.

After his eighty-eighth birthday, the time at which he had told me he planned to slip away, my father seemed to be doing just that. He lost his ability to walk, talk, or feed himself, and when my mother, always the can-do nurse, admitted that it was too taxing physically for her to care for him at home, we made a family decision to move him to the nursing home across town. It was as welcoming a place as it could be. His sister, Aunt Bev, was living across the hall, and the staff made sure the siblings had plenty of time together, holding hands and watching old-time movies each afternoon. One day, my friend Catharine, the harpist on the hospice floor in New York where I volunteered, loaded her harp into the back seat of a taxi and made the journey over the bridge to New Jersey to play for them.

When Evan and I finally arrived at the nursing home, the receptionist greeted us warmly as I signed the visitors log. "Your sister-in-law just took Bev for a walk outside. It's such a gorgeous day. Your mom is upstairs with your father now."

Evan and I headed straight for the third floor. At the threshold of my father's room, we paused. My brother David had positioned my father's bed to face the window, overlooking the trees. The window was open, and a warm breeze gently billowed the curtains. My mother was in an armchair pulled up close to the bed, holding my father's hand and looking at him intently. When she heard us, she turned in our direction. She looked startled.

"He just took his last breath," she said, astonished. "Only a minute ago I said the Twenty-third Psalm—*Yea, though I walk through the valley of the shadow of death*—and when I finished, he died. His body just stopped."

She looked so small, like a fragile bird. I ran to the bed and looked at my father. His eyes were open, but the force that animated his existence was unquestionably gone. I kissed his forehead, which was still warm to my lips. Tears were streaming down my face as I went to my mother. We were both sobbing softly and holding each other as Evan approached us, wrapping his arms around our shoulders. My son, now a young man, comforting both my mother and me.

"Mom," Evan would say to me later, as I recounted the scene aloud. "Do you have any idea how perfect that timing was? If we had arrived a moment earlier, Nana would have been asking how our trip was instead of paying complete attention to Pop-Pop. He already knew how much we loved him. It had to be exactly the way it was."

He was becoming such a wise soul, that Evan.

We held my father's memorial service on a crisp fall day at the lake where my father had grown up and where my brother David now lived with his family. Before the guests arrived, my brothers and I and our families hiked up the mountain overlooking the lake to scatter half of my father's ashes, just as he had wished. The rest were to go under the holly tree at the water's edge, where my grandparents' ashes were already buried.

I climbed to the highest ridge, with a clear view of my father's childhood home. Through the changing autumn leaves, I could also see Manhattan in the distance. It was almost too beautiful for the occasion. I stepped out onto a flat rocky outcropping and poured his ashes into the shape of a giant heart.

Back at the house, Aunt Bev, Mom, and a couple dozen close friends and family began to gather for the ceremony. My mother had asked me if I would lead the service. "As long as I can wear sunglasses the whole time," I told her, half joking. The truth was, I couldn't think of a better way to honor my father, and I was glad she had asked.

I changed quickly out of my jeans and hiking boots, called everyone to gather, and positioned myself beside the holly tree. My voice cracking, I began, "We are here to express gratitude for the man we called Dad, Dr. George, Hon, Pop-Pop, Bud . . ."

My mother sat in the front row, serene and nodding along. My brother George read a prayer my mother had written. The six grandchildren took turns reading lines from a song my parents liked. Then I asked our family members to come forward and place the handmade cards that we'd each created for my father, expressing the private thoughts of our hearts, into a spot my brother had dug next to the tree. The cover of my card was simply a line from Thoreau: *There is no remedy for love but to love more.* After Drew placed the last note into the ground, my mother sprinkled the remainder of my father's ashes on top of our offerings.

Afterward, everyone headed inside my brother's house. I lingered by the lake, sitting down heavily on a rock. I tossed a handful of small pebbles into the water and watched a cluster of concentric ripples expand out from the centers.

It felt like an hour had passed when Michelle, the sister-in-law of my late childhood friend Marisa, called out to me, "Barb, look at the colors." I turned to see where she was pointing. There in the sky, the setting sun cast a rainbow over the lake. To my aching heart, it felt like a sign—as my friend Consolee's rainbow over Central Park had to her—a reminder that, as my father had once promised me, "This too shall pass."

Ten days after my father's memorial service, my mother entered the hospital. My brother David had dropped by her house on his way to work and found her sitting on the living room couch, unable to breathe, a symptom of congestive heart failure. She was admitted to the cardiac-care unit at the hospital where my father and grandfather had worked and where my brother George had followed in their footsteps as a doctor.

When Drew was born, my mother had shown up at the door of our apartment with a suitcase in each hand. I hadn't been expecting her. Every inch of my body was trembling from exhaustion, and I was overjoyed to see her. "I'm not leaving you until you're ready for me to go," she said, stepping into the apartment.

That's exactly what I was drawn to do for her now. I sat down with Dave and the boys. "I don't want to have any regrets," I explained. "I want to be with her, however long I can be helpful." It didn't take any convincing. The next morning, I moved back into my childhood home with two suitcases of my own.

By night I slept in my old bedroom, then woke up early each morning to drive to my mother's bedside. Her hours were occupied by performing small acts of gratitude. She asked me to bring blank thank-you cards. Her handwriting was getting shakier, but she persevered in writing dozens of notes to loved ones, telling each personally what they meant to her. When a nurse advised us to take home any valuables my mother may have brought to the hospital so they would be secure, my mom responded with a laugh, "All of my valuables walk on two feet."

After my mother had spent a week in the hospital, social workers from the palliative-care and hospice teams came to sit with us. Her heart was failing, and she frequently coughed up an alarming amount of pink foamy mucus. It was clear that we had exhausted all of the treatments to forestall her condition and that she wasn't going to get better. While I knew that I had entered the world of hospice to prepare myself for my parents' eventual deaths, I felt blindsided by this moment of truth.

"My goal is to go home," she told the social workers weakly.

"We can make that happen quickly while giving you support to be as comfortable as possible," one of them replied. My entire family knew that hospice didn't mean "giving up on someone." Rather, we saw it as the most realistic, compassionate care available.

My brothers and I got to work setting up a hospital bed in my mother's living room, overlooking a mountain in the distance. It was the sunniest, most cheerful room of her house. We barely had time to move my father's things from the room where he had spent so many days. Now we were setting up a place where we knew my mother would eventually draw her last breath. My friend Julie brought over a magnificent poinsettia, and we arranged my mother's little porcelain manger scene in the window where she could see it easily, for the holidays were approaching.

We had all hoped my mother would feel somewhat rejuvenated at home, free from the middle-of-the-night monitoring and medicine and the all-hours broadcasts over the hospital paging system. But there was to be no such relief. Excruciating pain wracked her body, and I was suddenly thrust into the thick of caregiving. An aide and I would shift my mother every few hours to prevent bedsores, and she would cry out in agony. I rubbed her back and cleaned up after her when she vomited. I learned to monitor her oxygen tank. A home-hospice nurse taught me how to administer morphine and other sedatives under my mother's tongue from a box of color-coded medicines that they left in our refrigerator—blue syringe, yellow syringe, pink syringe, green syringe, each with a different purpose. In the face of her devastating anguish, I could see no silver lining, no virtue.

I had never seen a hospice patient in such agony. The doctors and nurses assigned to her care were observing her constantly, making sure they hadn't missed any underlying cause. It seemed so unfair that my mother, who had lived a life of kindness and service to others, had drawn this unlucky card. One aide came up with an explanation no one else mentioned. "It's called terminal agitation, sweetheart," she said gently. "I bet everyone is telling you that your mama is dying from a broken heart after your daddy died. But maybe she wanted to live."

I considered her words. My mother, without a doubt, wanted to live. She wanted to plant a Japanese maple tree in her yard in my father's memory, visit the shore with her grandchildren, and go back to volunteering in the local nursing home. She had plans, and death wasn't part of them. No wonder she was agitated.

When my mother had finally fallen asleep after one particularly bad episode, I put on a winter coat and told the aide I would be back soon. I walked across the street to the cemetery where I had spent countless hours as a kid. The cemetery was a benevolent place for our family; with its wide lawns and sunken markers, it was no surprise that visitors often mistook it for a park. "It's a wonderful place to live," my mother had always said of our home. "We have quiet neighbors."

My feet crunched on the frosted ground heading up the hill into the trees to the spot where the cemetery's staff discarded withering flowers. I took off my gloves and dialed my friend Dana, who had been checking in with me every day.

"Go ahead and cry," she said. "You don't need to explain anything at all. Wail if you want to. I'm here for you."

That did it. Being validated by Dana in every aspect of this journey, including the darkest moments, was a gift beyond measure. I started shaking, then crying. I rooted around for a tissue in my pocket but couldn't find one. The boys would call this ugly crying.

Between words, I stammered out my truth. How my mother looked more like a skeleton than a living person. That she was screaming out in pain, gasping for air, and calling out imploringly to God. I felt like I was seeing a new side to death, and my fury was rising. "I'm pissed off at the so-called angel of death, who seems to have lost directions to my town, even though he was here a couple of months ago for my father."

When Dana and I hung up and I returned to the house twenty minutes later, my mother was still sound asleep. I took a warm shower and turned on my laptop for the first time in a week. There were messages from family and friends, with offerings from the heart. Christians and Jews prayed for my mother and our family. A Hindu friend led an *aarti* ceremony, lighting oil candles and offering prayers for her well-being. There were Buddhist chants and gifts of poetry by Rumi. Generous Bear did a sacred pipe ceremony for our family and the professionals caring for my mom. It was as if my mother had become everyone's mother.

On the afternoon that the hospice nurse told us that Mom likely had one day to live, Dave and I spoke to the boys. They had seen her the week before, on Thanksgiving, and presented her with homemade cards telling her how much she meant to them. But it didn't seem like enough. I remembered a friend from Guinea once telling me of his village's tradition: "We don't hide the moment of death from the young people. Everyone comes and sits at the bedside."

We offered the option to the boys. "Think about this carefully—the decision is up to you, and there's no right or wrong thing to do. Nana is not responding anymore, but maybe she can still hear us. If you want to come sit with us until the end, we will be by your side." They both said yes.

When they arrived, though, I was afraid we had made a mistake. The boys took one look at her body, now about eighty pounds. The angular bones under her skin seemed to take over the familiar face we had known. She was not conscious of their presence, at least outwardly. Both boys started to cry silently. I shot Dave a worried look. Drew walked out of the room, and Dave followed him. A few minutes later they rejoined us, and we all pulled up chairs around the bed and held hands. Assuming my mother could hear us, we recounted our favorite moments with her and my dad. And when whoever was talking stopped, we sat silently until someone else was moved to speak. Throughout the day we were joined by her best friend—Marisa's mother—and her sister, my brothers and their families, and the minister from her church. The boys witnessed adults get choked up and hug one another and kiss a dying woman and comb her hair and adjust her blankets. *We learn to say goodbye by listening and watching,* I thought. *By bearing witness.*

That night, my brothers slept on the living room floor, near my mother's bed, wanting to be attentive to her every need. Dave, the boys, and I crawled into my parents' bed, asking my brothers to awaken us if anything changed. My body was drained from weeks of poor sleep, and I felt a soft reassurance in lying close to my family, so full of health and energy.

The next morning, the hospice nurse arrived to check my mother's vitals. She was amazed that she had made it through the night. If this were truly my mother's last hour on earth, what would she want, I wondered. I went up to the attic and rooted around for the little circular candle holder my mother used to mark the Sundays leading up to Christmas. It was my mother's favorite ritual of the year, when we sat together as a family, lighting candles, singing, and reading passages from the Bible.

We were a couple of days shy of the first official Sunday of the holiday season, but I couldn't see it being a mistake to start early. I called everyone around my mother's bed. We sang every Christmas song we knew—my Jewish kids and husband, an atheist, and a few who weren't sure what they believed.

The moment before we lit the candles, we remembered that there was a tank of oxygen in the room and we put the matches away. We didn't need the light—light was present in that room like I had never witnessed before. It came in the form of pure, clear love. It was our love for my mother and for my father too. It expressed itself in a glowing warmth that we could palpably feel between all of us gathered. It was present in every honest gesture, every tear, every bit of laughter. There was so much love

With my parents, at home in New Jersey
(Photograph by Debra Baida)

in that room that it began to gently undo the twisted knots of pain that had come before it.

An hour after our makeshift service, my mother drew her final breath. At long last, she looked at peace. Slowly, I rose to do what I had witnessed many times over on the hospice floor. I took petals from an arrangement of flowers on the mantelpiece and scattered them gently on the sheet that covered her body. My brother George tucked a small picture of his daughter, who was away at college, among the petals so she could be near my mom too, like all of the other grandchildren who came trickling in.

Several weeks after my mother died, a large rectangular box arrived at our door. I could see that it was from my friend Lisa in North Carolina, who had been holding space for the loss that had been unfolding in my family, through calls and messages.

I opened it carefully with the kitchen scissors and pulled out a large framed painting. It was a scene of three children playing in a garden, which Lisa had asked her children's art teacher to paint for me. A girl with long blond braids, as I had as a child, was jumping rope. One boy was sitting in the grass with his back against the trunk of a tree; the other was swinging from a rope swing. In the distance, on a dock overlooking a lake, sat an elderly couple, watching the setting sun.

Across the bottom of the painting were my mother's words. *All of my valuables walk on two feet.*

THE HOUSE ON HURON ROAD

In the months after my parents died, my brothers and I prepared to sell their home. All three of us had grown up in that modest 1960s-era house tucked into the woods on a quiet cul-de-sac. I was not prepared for how profoundly the process would affect me. Once my mother's ashes joined my father's under the holly tree by the lake, my childhood home felt as if it were a physical proxy for them. Now it too was about to be gone from our lives.

My father chose where we would live by studying aerial photographs of the New York/New Jersey metropolitan area. Our town marked the boundary where urban streets gave way to woods and wide-open fields. This decidedly green land would be our home. Like many towns in the area, it eventually saw more development than my parents had ever anticipated, but the place I remember from childhood had apple orchards and a working dairy farm that delivered fresh milk in glass bottles.

My father believed you could never have enough trees and went to work planting even more on our property, including a Japanese maple in memory of his father, which I could see blowing delicately outside my bedroom window. Chipmunks made a home under a gazebo, and cardinals frolicked in the birdbath in my mother's wildflower garden. My father was so exuberant about our corner of paradise that he had our yard certified as a wildlife habitat by an environmental organization and proudly hung the rectangular metal plaque on a little wooden well that adorned our front lawn.

The house disappeared from our lives in stages. First there were the possessions within. My sister-in-law wept when she handed over a bag of my mother's shoes to a Goodwill cashier, as I had done when I dropped my father's eyeglasses in a box for those in need. Shoes and eyeglasses . . . I had never before considered how intimate the articles of the everyday could be.

It was my brother who found the little Hallmark calendar my mother used to keep track of the significant events of the myriad people in her life. It was quintessential Mom. A Star of David drawn on a fall day was a reminder to send cards to me, Dave, and the boys, and to my in-laws, Marvin and Laura, for the Jewish new year. A little arrow pointing up meant someone died and went to heaven that day.

One little arrow on December 1 was how my brother figured out that my mother had died on the same date as her own mother, our grandmother, in the same house. Looking over his shoulder, I was moved by the connection. *Same date, same place.* I remembered that Mac's wife Annie too had died on the same date, in the same room, as her own mother eleven years earlier. I shivered a little.

My parents, who had been born into the Great Depression, embodied frugality, and their home reflected it. I had inherited their gene for all things practical. Besides my mother's desk, a cardboard box overflowing with family photographs, and a painting of birch trees from their dining room, I found myself taking only useful things—a stapler, Ziploc bags, a paring knife, and the *I Love You* pillowcases my mother had bought for my childhood bed one Christmas.

One night, after a long day of sorting things into piles of Keep, Donate, Sell, or Discard, my brother David threw together a meal from what little remained. Linguini with clam sauce from a can, a bottle of red wine, and a bar of my father's favorite dark chocolate (72 percent cacao, he always insisted). We toasted my parents and sat down to eat off their simple plates with plain utensils in their kitchen with the dated sunflower wallpaper we teased them for without mercy. It may have been the most satisfying meal I've ever had.

When the house was finally empty, we sought out real estate agents. One told us no one these days wanted to live in a house on a wooded lot when they could have a large lawn. Her observation felt like a denunciation of our parents' greatest source of joy, and we rejected her immediately. Another admired the house for its bones. "It's perfect for the right family," he said. We shook hands on the spot.

"Are you sure you don't want to live there?" my mom's sister asked one last time. "You, Dave, and the boys are outdoorsy. You could move out of the city . . ." But I knew the house on Huron Road wasn't my life anymore. It was time to let it go.

After we closed the front door with the brass knocker for the last time, I looked at my brother, who was smiling sheepishly. "What did you do?" I asked, sensing his impishness.

"I just hid a tiny picture of them in the rafters of the attic, where the new owners will never find them," he said. "It won't hurt anyone, right?" he asked. I gave him a high five.

A year after the house sold, my brother was eating at a local restaurant with friends. He noticed that the couple at the next table was staring at him. It became so obvious that my brother leaned over to them to break the ice. "I'm sorry," he said, "but do I know you from somewhere?"

"Yes! We bought your parents' house!" the woman exclaimed. "And we want you to know how much we love it. The hardwood floors, the gazebo, the little well with the wildlife-habitat sign out front."

My brother wondered if they had found the picture in the attic, but he decided not to ask.

My parents didn't visit me in my dreams for over a year after they were gone. It was okay, though, because a few months before she died, my mother had a dream that she told me about one morning while sitting at her kitchen table, sipping hot water from a mug.

"You were out back, cooking something on the barbecue," she began. I pictured myself at the grill downstairs, right outside the sliding glass door.

The gazebo on Huron Road

"I was upstairs in my bathrobe, not feeling so well," she continued. "All of a sudden you were screaming, because a big bear had come up to you and you were afraid." She looked more animated than I had seen her in a while.

"So you know what I did?" she asked. "I came running downstairs to you so fast it felt like I was flying. I went outside, picked you up in my arms—as big as you are now—and carried you back into the house, where you were completely safe."

That was all the confirmation I had ever needed—that the house, my mother, my father too, could defy the limits of physicality and time. No load would be too heavy, no staircase insurmountable. Nothing can separate us from those we love—not even death. With the memory of the decades we had together sustaining me, I took my first steps forward without them. And when I did, our relationship simply shifted into a new formless form.

BARBARA

A few years after my father's medical school friend Sherwin Nuland won the National Book Award for *How We Die,* he confessed to a reporter what had concerned him about being honored for bringing death out of the shadows: "You know, buddy, what situation you put yourself into?" he had asked himself. "You've got to die as an example to others. You've got to have 'the good death.' You have to be brave. You have to be courageous."

Shep's comment stopped me in my tracks. Would I now face a similar conundrum for having written about death?

As it inevitably will, being intimate with the mortality of others led me straight to confronting my own eventual death. How would I handle it? Would I feel brave and courageous, weak and terrified, all of the above and everything in between? Or, if my life were to end abruptly, would I have even an inkling of those feelings?

In recent years, I have had small glimpses of my own mortality. Three times I brushed up against the threat of breast cancer, a disease that runs among the women in my family. Each time, as a serious-looking doctor showed me the point of concern on the mammogram and sonogram imaging, Marisa came to mind, with her head bald, in a hospital gown, legs dangling from the edge of the examining table, saying almost cheerfully, "What news do you have for me today, Doc?" What she had endured, physically and mentally, with grace and often with a sense of humor, felt superhuman to me.

After each of my resulting biopsies, I saved my hospital wristband and placed it next to my meditation cushion at home. As the days passed and I awaited the results, I watched the ups and downs of my mind: *sickness/health, frightened/brave, beginning/ end.* Why did I do this to myself, pitting everything against an opposite, causing me to respond as if in constant battle? I reminded myself that I was capable of more subtlety than that and tried to move without judgment in the space between the tension.

A few times during the medical scares, I had the experience of what felt like arriving at a home base, a peaceful place where I was completely aware of my wildly fluctuating feelings without being caught up in them. While this too was fleeting, it reminded me that uncertainties and obstacles can nudge us into waking up a little, if we let them. That there is a productive way of being in which we can face the life we have instead of pining for the life we'd rather have. I wouldn't go so far as to call it "acceptance," for I was given a clean bill of health each time and returned to life as I knew it, on-my-knees grateful and relieved.

I humbly submit that I still have work to do.

So I start with the small things. I treat everyday goodbyes—to work, school, the grocery store around the corner—with consequence. I say "I love you" more and try never to pass up an opportunity to express genuine gratitude. I work hard to show up for others, ever watchful of the ways I might rather separate instead. I am a better listener. I know that tears do not need to be hastily wiped away or apologized for. When I'm suffering from the flu or hobbling around with a broken toe, I try to use it as an opportunity to explore just how fragile, how tenuous, our bodies can be. I try to not take it personally.

The journey of life and loss has changed me, deepened me. I employ a deceptively small question when faced with decisions of all levels of magnitude: *What would you do if you had only one year left to live?* That gets to our priorities quickly, I've learned.

That same question led me to a most unexpected decision one morning in New York City. At midlife, wondering where this voyage would take me next, I decided that if I had a limited number of days remaining, I'd like to devote them to exploring even further the question of what gives meaning to our lives, what elevates our existence.

In our culture, we are told that death is the last and greatest taboo—as welcome as a skunk at a garden party. Yet most often when I spoke of my experiences with loss, people opened up about their own. Death truly is a great equalizer, it turns out. As I sat with stories of grief and suffering, I began to hear an undercurrent of the inner resources people drew upon when their lives got hard. How people evolve and grow, even as the body withers. How we fare better when our sense of meaning is big enough to hold the things that don't make sense. Every person, whether they defined themselves as religious, spiritual, agnostic, or atheist, made me even more curious about the ways in which we seek comfort and purpose, especially when we find ourselves in the crucible of our lives. Aren't we, to borrow from William Faulkner, not meant to merely endure but to prevail?

With this in mind, I enrolled in a unique interfaith seminary. I was far more interested in the content of the classes than the outcome, which was becoming an ordained interfaith member of the clergy. I had absolutely no intention of having a congregation. I respected everyone's quests to make meaning, whether it involved some form of belief or none at all. I had found a place for free-thinkers, though, and I too—an older version of my childhood self who had often climbed my parents' bookcase to reach my father's colorful set of books on the world's religions—longed to immerse myself in the glorious diversity of sacred wisdom.

Dave understood from the start what this newest step in my quest was all about.

"Barb, I get what you are doing. It's not about religion or about you becoming a reverend."

"What is it, then?" I asked.

"It's about walking with more reverence in your life, every single day."

I reached over to touch his arm, grateful that he understood me so well—sometimes even better than I understood myself.

Dave, it turned out, was right. My time in seminary confirmed what I had learned about loss and life: that living with the end in mind can be an ennobling endeavor. That the more we embrace dying, the more we embrace living. That life was never meant to be about our self-interests but about being a source of love for others. That our presence is far more important than any technical know-how we may possess about religion or spirituality. That compassion and generosity of spirit will prevail over rigid thoughts and beliefs every single time. That sitting with discomfort can be far more intimate and helpful than trying to fix that which is unfixable. And that when something can be remedied, we must not allow ourselves to become passive but rather step in and fill the void. All of this is the essence of reverence.

After two years of spiritual explorations, on the day of our ordination at Manhattan's majestic Riverside Church, I glanced down the row at my classmates' vestments. Each person wore a stole of their own choosing around their neck, and the rainbow of colors and elaborate patterns added to the festive atmosphere. My own stole was a long piece of black cloth, upon which over four hundred white antique buttons were arranged like a meandering stream of water. The artist I found online who had created it told me that she liked to sit and fasten on the buttons in the quiet evenings, imaging that they had traveled on journeys at sea, attended funerals, weddings, births. It perfectly represented what I felt about the interconnectedness of all beings, throughout place and time.

The French author Jules Renard once wrote: *If I had my life to live over again, I would ask that not a thing be changed, but that*

With Chodo at my ordination
Riverside Church, New York City

my eyes be opened wider. Wider, I would add, to *every* reality—
not just to the happiness but to every heartache too.

My ever-expanding journey has led to this place. I know at
times I'll stumble along, half asleep. But I also know I can wake
up and find my way again. We all can. It's called a life worth
living. I get it. I understand. It is enough.

POSTSCRIPT: HEARTWOOD

The trees. In the end, it always seemed to come back to the trees.

A global pandemic had reached our shores, and the New York City area found itself an epicenter. Covid-19 notably crept its way into vulnerable nursing homes, taking from us a disproportionate number of our elders. Aunt Bev was one of them.

My brother David had called me from her bedside, where he'd been given the option to don personal protective equipment and say goodbye in person. For months we had been unable to visit her because the facility was under strict lockdown, and we were all missing her so much it hurt. Just as he had leapt in the car years ago and driven hours to be by her side when we suspected she had fallen, he once again did not hesitate to go to her.

Over speakerphone, I could hear his reassuring voice, muffled through his mask. "Aunt Bev, Barbara is here now too. We're both right here with you." He held the phone near her ear, and I could hear her shallow breathing. My instinct was to hold her hand—nothing in my training had prepared me to be with the dying from such a distance. *Stay present,* I willed myself.

"We love you very much, Aunt Bev," I began. "We want to

thank you for everything." My brother and I took turns, expressing our gratitude for the countless ways she had showed up for us and for others in her lifetime. We talked about her childhood at the lake, of moving to a Navy training base with her parents after the attack on Pearl Harbor, of her years teaching college students, of vacations with our family. When she fidgeted, we guided her through a scan of her body. "Relax your forehead, Aunt Bev. Let go of the muscles behind your eyes, in your jaw . . ." Time slowed, and I felt myself easing into the relaxation too.

A nurse came in and told my brother the time was up. What had felt like spacious hours at Aunt Bev's bedside was really under an hour, and we had to leave her. How do you say a final good-bye at a time like this? My brother and I did the only thing we could think of—we placed her in the care of those who had gone before her. "Bud and Alice are nearby," we told her of our father and mother. "Mother, Father too," we said, referencing our grandparents. I added her favorite dog, Laddie, for good measure. "They're right here for you," my brother said. "And they love you like we do." Her breathing was imperceptible over the phone. I had a new realization that with Aunt Bev dying, my brothers and I would move up some invisible ladder—now we would be the elders of the family. My brother gave Aunt Bev's hand a final squeeze with his gloved one.

"We did the best we could," I told him when he got back into the car. While it was unlike any farewell I had ever experienced, I knew that it was true. We can do extraordinary things when we lead with love.

Aunt Bev died the following morning. While she had no one at her bedside, I had the unshakable feeling that she hadn't been alone. When it would be safe to gather again, we would hold a small memorial service for her beside the holly tree at the lake.

But first I would be part of another memorial service.

I was invited as an interfaith minister to give a blessing at the burial being held at New York City's potter's field on Hart Island, an uninhabited strip of land off the Bronx in the Long Island Sound. Facing escalating deaths, the city used the land as a public cemetery for men and women whose bodies would not be claimed for private burial. One minister I knew had lost forty-four members of his congregation, most of whom came from underserved communities and performed jobs that made them disproportionately vulnerable to the virus. Like them, so many people who were being interred on Hart Island had already experienced incalculable hardship and discrimination in life.

The memorial service was to be virtual, with only the city's chaplain having a permit to be physically present. He trained the camera of his cell phone on a simple granite memorial dedicated to the over one million people who had been buried there since 1869. Stones and pebbles had been placed on the top of the monument, borrowing from a Jewish custom to show respect for the dead.

The ceremony was centered on interfaith prayers that matched the diversity of those who had died. I had written a blessing to acknowledge the original people who inhabited the island, long before it was obtained through a treaty with a moneyed landowner. Generous Bear had taught me to always pay respect to those who had come before. The stars, he reminded me, were campfires of the ancestors. I also gave thanks to the wind, the water, the sky, and Mother Earth, for embracing her children who were being returned to this sacred ground. "She receives them all equally," I said, "regardless of where they were from or the circumstances that brought them here."

As I spoke, I could see whitecaps on the water and birds flying in and out of the camera frame. There was a wild beauty to the scene, and it felt more alive than dead. The memorial was short but long enough to convey that, along with the pain and injustice that was the story of so many of the deceased, there was also a humbling sense of their fundamental dignity and worth. A line of tall trees blew in the distance as if bowing in unison— the heartwood of Hart Island.

One final story, one final tree.

When I was seventeen, my father took our family to England to meet Maureen's parents, sisters, and her sisters' children. I was so enthralled by the prospect of visiting the fairy-tale land where Lady Diana and Prince Charles had married a few years earlier that I didn't give much thought to just how out of the ordinary our family pilgrimage was. It was, after all, over two decades since Maureen had fallen off the boat into the glassy waters of the Housatonic River.

Looking back on it now from the age my parents were at the time, I see that my father conceived of the trip as an opportunity to demonstrate his connection and loyalty to both families, ours and Maureen's. My mother quietly turned her attention to calling a travel agent and booking flights. Later she told me that she had made a decision to swallow any misgivings and discomfort she felt about this journey for the higher benefit of providing my father the healing he still needed.

We arrived by train in High Wycombe, the rolling countryside northwest of London where Maureen's parents lived in the brick house that had been Maureen's childhood home. I remember a narrow shopping street nearby lined with parked cars that seemed miniature in size. Everything felt foreign, quaint even.

Maureen's mother came out of the house to greet us and stood silently, her lips imitating a smile as the five of us approached her front step. She eyed George, David, and me, perhaps thinking of the grandchildren she would have had if Maureen had lived. Maureen's father handled our presence differently. He kissed both my mother and me, gave my brothers firm handshakes, then shook my father's hand hard, and pulled him into a warm embrace.

My mother and father had tea with Maureen's parents while her sisters' kids entertained the rest of us upstairs. I remember nothing more than awkward teen attempts to find common ground. No one wanted to talk about the royal wedding of Prince Charles and Lady Diana anymore, it seemed. "Do you play any sports?" the kids asked my brothers, who tentatively shook their heads no. "You don't play football?" they asked incredulously. Something about the rivalry between England and France that was in no way part of our worldview. At least we knew enough to understand that they were talking about soccer.

After a while, my father called up to us and asked us to come downstairs. Maureen's father led the way through the back door and into a small yard lined by a row of hedges. In the center stood a single ash tree. It seemed a tree like any other, at first glance.

"What do you see up there?" Maureen's father asked, turning toward me. All eyes, mine included, gazed upward. I had no answer for him. My mother, shielding her eyes from the high summer sun, spotted it first. "My goodness, this tree is full of roses!" I squinted as well and it came slowly into focus: Dozens upon dozens of pink roses bloomed throughout the leafy green canopy, each flower boldly standing out against a bright-blue sky.

Maureen's mother looked down at her shoes and brushed her eyes with the back of her fingers. Maureen's father said, "When Maureen returned to the house after the wedding, she placed cuttings from her wedding bouquet right into the ground beneath this tree. They took root here in the sunlight." Suddenly I remembered the photograph of Maureen and her father walking through the churchyard cemetery, the bouquet of rosebuds and lilies of the valley flowing gracefully from her hands. Maureen's father knelt by the base of the tree and ran his fingers over the soil. "With a little careful tending, we have roses every year."

My mother's eyes filled with tears. It was as if I could see her enormous heart reaching even further than it had at our journey's genesis. "Your English Rose," she said, looking kindly at Maureen's mother.

"I am so happy George married you," Maureen's father said, hugging my mother. Maureen's mother looked up and nodded ever so perceptibly.

I think of that tree often, of its deep roots, strong branches, and verdant canopy. But most of all, I think of the heartwood within and what it represents in my life. The core of that miraculous tree, the center of which has expanded over the years to include not only Maureen but her parents and mine and so many others—strong enough to give life to all who have come after. Through them I have come to understand myself, to stand firm and purposeful yet flexible enough to sway with the prevailing winds of life.

I have no true understanding about what happens to us when we die. But I do believe this: Just as a tree is made up of its life and its death, its beginning and its end, so too are we. Someday, in time and with a little grace, each of us, in our individual lives, will form heartwood. And in the very forming, we will sustain those who come after us. I will be heartwood for someone someday. As will Dave, as will Evan and Drew. And if the boys choose to have children, my grandchildren too in the distant future will become heartwood, embraced by the ever-expanding growth rings around them. It's all so natural, both common and transcendent when it comes right down to it.

But there's one more thing. If we do it well, if we carefully tend to our lives, watering the soil, minding the thorns, and nourishing the memories of our loved ones, we may come to understand grieving as a beautiful expression of love. And someday, that love may even bear roses.

acknowledgments

My gratitude begins with you, the readers who opened to the first page of *Heartwood* and came with me on a journey of loss and love. In our death-shy culture, sharing these stories matters. You give me hope.

At the heart of this book are the family, friends, and hospice patients I've been able to companion for even a short time at the end of their lives. I am humbled by all of them. To each of their loved ones who allowed me to be a part of their story, I thank you. Special thanks go to Dave Donati and the entire Palladino family, Gary Vineberg and Cathy Clark, Jon Drescher, and the Bell family.

I would also like to acknowledge the hospice workers, volunteers, and family members everywhere who show up to do the work of caregiving day after day. In particular, I offer gratitude to the Visiting Nurse Service of New York, which provided me with training and a place to offer my own service as a volunteer.

It truly takes a village to write a book. I think back to the earliest days when Debra Baida and Sven Eberlein sat me down in front of a computer and instructed me to start blogging on my year-to-live experiment. Cindy Cooper nudged me along gently with well-timed questions and a place to share my first chapter with others in her living room. It was Whitney Frick, whose heartfelt enthusiasm for the story of my friendship with Marisa—first published on the wonderful website *Modern Loss*—first set this book in motion. And the ever-wise Arielle Eckstut led me to my intrepid agent, Miriam Altshuler of DeFiore and Company. Miriam not only guided me assiduously through the long road to publishing but was one step ahead of me on the parenting journey and generously shared her sage advice on both fronts.

I found my publishing home at Flatiron Books under the vision of Bob Miller and my editor, Sarah Murphy. Sarah has an extraordinary instinct for getting to the core of writing and understood in an instant what *Heartwood* was about. She gave me permission to invite death in through the front door, even as I was trying to force it through the back. I'm beyond grateful to the wisdom of Bryn Clark, Megan Lynch, and Lauren Bittrich, as well as to Sydney Jeon, at Flatiron, who made the process a pleasurable one.

To my writing companions, Jane Praeger and Lynn Love. Over the years, our trio has gotten together for countless calls, writing sessions, and self-styled retreats. Our relationship has been such a gift of truth-telling and friendship.

In a category unto himself is my dear friend Allston James, author, playwright, painter, and professor. He and his partner, Rachel Weintraub, and I spent many hours at the Rubin Museum café, tirelessly poring over the details of our lives. I'm indebted to them both for the love, the listening, and the lattes.

I give thanks to the dear friends who offered their encouragement and expertise over the years. I'm especially grateful to John Charles Thomas for his eagle eye and humor, and to Emily Russell, who has the priceless combination of an enormous heart and an intellect to match. The years of my life are nourished by my college friends Lisa Goldberg, Joy Stankowski, Lisa Clancy, Jessica Barest, and Shuchi Stanger. To Merle Kailas, Carolyn Barber, Matthew DeMaio, Nancy Lasher, Jordan Hamowy, Laurie Gwen Shapiro, Tina Rosenberg, Scott Drosselmeier, Nomi Naeem, Lisa Williams, and Rich Jacovitz—you were so kind to let me talk your ears off! Endless appreciation to the entire Zier family. I am so charmed by the wit, warmth, and wisdom of the Jell-O Fellows and their partners, especially Jayne Riew, a beautiful creative soul who so generously read the earliest chapters of the book.

The word *frolleagues* was invented for the friends and colleagues I've met who are committed to justice and to the well-being of all. Thank you to the laureates and trustees of the Civil Courage Prize and to all of the activists and nonprofit organizations I've been privileged to work with for over twenty-five years. My respect for Consolee Nishimwe knows no bounds. Special thanks goes to my friend and EqualShot partner, Susan Wynn Kayne, and to the breakfast bunch: Jill Savitt, Amy Richards, and Julie Kay. My graduate school companions have never once turned down a call of distress or delight, especially Dana Buhl, Lisa Forehand, Susan Gibson, Angela Scaperlanda Buján, and Yasmin Fadlu-Deen. Sue Jaye Johnson and Kim

Sillen are both activists and artists whose creative work incorporates many media—thank you for everything. My endless appreciation goes to Anne Hoyt, Jessica Feierman, Mikaela Seligman, Karen Gladbach, and Viviana Waisman, who kept me belly-laughing even when we were stumbling up hills on the Camino de Santiago.

I am grateful to the entire One Spirit Interfaith Seminary community. From my classmates in the Class on Fire, to all of the talented and heart-centered faculty and staff who became my friends and colleagues once I became a dean, to the students I have had the privilege to companion along their journeys, I thank you. Special thanks to the most remarkable group of reverends for their well-timed advice, especially Diane Berke, Sarah Bowen, Elizabeth Friend-Ennis, Dave Munro, Gwendolyn Adam, Catharine DeLong, Jennifer Bailey, Melissa Stewart, Leslie Reambeault, and Susan Turchin. For Rev. David Wallace, who has traveled his own path of love and loss with an open heart and a willingness to give of himself, my journey would not have been complete without you. Rev. Martha Dewing, who starts each morning with the question "Who can I love today?"—I love you truly, madly, deeply.

I've also learned from some terrific teachers . . . Amy Cunningham, Barbara Joshin O'Hara, Sunita Viswanath and the Sadhana coalition, Joan Sadika Block, Murshida Khadija Goforth, Mirabai Starr, and the late Annmarie Zhati Agosta, who welcomed me so warmly on my first visit to the Nur Ashki Jerrahi Sufi Order. Thank you too to Judson Memorial Church and to Revs. Donna Schaper, Micah Bucey, and Valerie Holly, all of whom I came to know and respect while serving as a community minister. I am also grateful to the Disaster Spiritual Care team of the American Red Cross–Greater New York as well as the New York Disaster Interfaith Services.

My life has been blessed with many deep relationships, especially my spiritual soul sisters Michelle Bissanti, Annie Gilson, Vera Smith, and Beth Berman, as well as her son, the composer Jeff Berman, who taught me about the sounds of heartwood. To the contemplative communities and exemplars who have nourished my heart: the Insight Meditation Society, Dhamma Dhara, Dr. Daniel P. Brown, and the late masters Rahob Rinpoche Thupten Kalsang and His Holiness the 33rd Menri Trizin, spiritual leader of the Bön Tibetan tradition. I also want to thank the Zen Peacemakers and my friends in the Lakota bearing-witness community: Violet Catches, Manny Iron Hawk, and Renee Fasthorse-Iron Hawk. Claudia Iron Hawk—I am watching with excitement as your star rises!

A deep bow to Sensei Koshin Paley Ellison and Sensei Robert Chodo Campbell. What you have created through the New York Zen Center for Contemplative Care is a model for how we can move forward with presence in the dance of life and death. I don't have words to thank you for all I have learned from you.

Family is my truest treasure. My brothers, George and David, embody the very best of everything we learned from our parents, and I see that goodness reflected in their children—Anna, Cate, Kaia, and Forrest. I'm especially grateful that my brothers brought into my life my sisters-in-law, Alyssa and Suzanne, who will sit and cry with you with abandon, anywhere, any day of the week. And I give thanks for my in-laws, Marvin and Laura; my amazing sister-in-law, Marla; her children, Aaron and Talia; and Dave's dynamic extended family from coast to coast and across the Atlantic.

And, finally, to Dave and the boys—you are my tree, my roots, my branches, and my roses.

Evan and Drew, I often reflect on the countless ways in which you honored Nana and Pop-Pop. They would be so proud of every act of unconditional kindness you show to others, because, when it comes right down to it, that's the point of everything. Mainly, I wrote this book for you.

Dave, my love . . . it was you who could go deep with me on the biggest questions of meaning and purpose, while also calmly handling the quotidian of life—like toilet training the boys while I was away on meditation retreats. I know by now that there are no guarantees for longevity, but my greatest wish is living to a ripe old age with you, sitting in rocking chairs on that porch somewhere.

notes

xiii **newer growth sustain it:** "Anatomy of a Tree," Arbor Day Foundation, accessed October 30, 2020, https://www.arborday.org/trees/treeguide/anatomy.cfm.

3 **re-prioritizing goals and values:** Kenneth E. Vail, III, Jacob Juhl, Jamie Arndt, Matthew Vess, Clay Routledge, and Bastiaan T. Rutjens, "When Death Is Good for Life: Considering the Positive Trajectories of Terror Management," *Personality and Social Psychology Review*, published online on April 5, 2012, https://journals.sagepub.com/doi/10.1177/1088868312440046.

3 **It is Life's change agent:** Commencement address delivered by Steve Jobs, CEO of Apple Computer and of Pixar Animation Studios, on June 12, 2005, Stanford University, accessed June 22, 2020, https://news.stanford.edu/news/2005/june15/jobs-061505.html.

9 **rituals of the Druids:** Thomas W. Laqueur, "Beneath the Yew Tree's Shade," *The Paris Review*, October 31, 2015, https://www.theparisreview.org/blog/2015/10/31/beneath-the-yew-trees-shade/.

13 **and to have loved:** Sherwin Nuland, email message to author, April 18, 2013.

23 **the President of the United States:** Janny Scott, *A Singular Woman: The Untold Story of Barack Obama's Mother* (New York: Riverhead Books, 2011), 353.

31 **being diagnosed with cancer:** "The Psychological Impact of Infertility and Its Treatment," *Harvard Mental Health Letter*, accessed June 22, 2020, https://www.health.harvard.edu/newsletter_article/The-psychological-impact-of-infertility-and-its-treatment.

56   **If death has any value:** "Death," Patra Patra Chosnyid Sky-bamedpa, accessed November 2, 2020, http://www.meherb abadnyana.net/life_eternal/Book_One/Death.htm; http://www .meherbabadnyana.net/life_eternal/Copyrights.html.

57   **You at times travel:** Ibid.

60   **on a cold, wet evening:** Edward Waldo Emerson, *Henry Thoreau, as Remembered by a Young Friend* (New York: Houghton Mifflin, 1917), 116–117.

60   **so much pleasure and peace:** Ibid., 117.

60   **One world at a time:** "Henry David Thoreau," Poetry Foundation, accessed June 21, 2020, https://www.poetryfoundation.org /poets/henry-david-thoreau.

99   **at the time of your death:** Joan Halifax Roshi, "The Nine Contemplations of Atisha," Upaya Zen Center, accessed June 21, 2020, https://www.upaya.org/dox/Contemplations.pdf.

101   **became instantly enlightened:** "Buddhism: The Essential Points," a talk by Joseph Goldstein, April 9, 2013, Vimalakirti Centre of Buddhist Meditation, accessed June 22, 2020, http://www.vimalakirti .org/wp-content/uploads/2013/05/Joseph-essential-points.pdf.

125   **children were slaughtered:** Frederick Robertson Jones, "The Colonization of the Middle States and Maryland," in *The History of North America,* Vol. IV, ed. Guy Carleton Lee (Philadelphia: George Barrie & Sons, 1904), 33.

126   **prostitutes at Corlears Hook:** David L. Gold, *Studies in Etymology and Etiology: With Emphasis on Germanic, Jewish, Romance and Slavic Languages* (Alicante, Spain: Publicaciones de la Universidad de Alicante, 2009), 110.

126   **a two-month period of time:** Samuel Akerley, *Reports of Hospital Physicians: and Other Documents in Relation to the Epidemic Cholera*, ed. Dudley Atkins (New York: Board of Health, 1832), 112–149.

129 **disdain for hers:** "Lost Bird of Wounded Knee," South Dakota Public Broadcasting, accessed June 21, 2020, https://sdpb.sd.gov /Lostbird/summary.asp.

131 **apologize to the Lakota descendants:** Brendan O'Brien and Stephanie Keith, "Great-Great-Grandson of Wounded Knee Commander Asks for Forgiveness," Reuters, November 7, 2019, https:// www.reuters.com/article/us-usa-apology-nativeamericans/great -great-grandson-of-wounded-knee-commander-asks-for-forgiveness -idUSKBN1XI05I.

143 **long-lost loved ones:** Associated Press, "Near Death, Seeing Dead People May Be Neither Rare Nor Eerie," *U.S. News & World Report,* July 7, 2018, https://www.usnews.com/news/healthiest -communities/articles/2018-07-07/near-death-seeing-dead-people -may-be-neither-rare-nor-eerie.

182 **you have to be courageous:** Sherwin Nuland, "Facing Death," interview by Web of Stories, segment 55, audio 00:01, https://www .webofstories.com/play/sherwin.nuland/55.

190 **vulnerable to the virus:** Catherine E. Shoichet and Daniel Burke, "This New York Pastor Says His Parish Lost 44 People to Coronavirus," CNN, May 2020, https://www.cnn.com/interactive/2020 /05/us/new-york-church-coronavirus-deaths-cnnphotos/.

191 **with a moneyed landowner:** Allison C. Meier, "Pandemic Victims Are Filling NYC's Hart Island. It Isn't the First Time," *National Geographic,* April 13, 2020, https://www.nationalgeographic.com /history/2020/04/unclaimed-coronavirus-victims-being-buried-on -hart-island-long-history-as-potters-field/#close//www.vimalakirti .org/wp-content/uploads/2013/05/Joseph-essential-points.pdf.

about the author

Barbara Becker is a writer and ordained interfaith minister who has dedicated more than twenty-five years to partnering with human rights advocates around the world in pursuit of peace and interreligious understanding. She has worked with the United Nations, Human Rights First, the Ms. Foundation for Women, and the Grameen Bank of Bangladesh, and has participated in a delegation of Zen Peacemakers and Lakota elders in the sacred Black Hills of South Dakota. She has sat with hundreds of people at the end of their lives and views each as a teacher. Through writing, she explores what it means to live a life of meaning. Barbara lives in New York City with her interfaith family. More at barbarabecker.com.